The Watkins Kitchen
Collection

Winona, Minnesota
Winnipeg, Manitoba

Pepper

THE WATKINS KITCHEN COLLECTION

WRITING AND CREATIVE DESIGN
Jeff Severson

RECIPE DEVELOPMENT AND TESTING
Rita Bechly

DESIGN AND ILLUSTRATION
The Green Edge
Burgandy Nilles

ART DIRECTION
Terri Lieder, Watkins Incorporated
The Green Edge

FOOD PHOTOGRAPHY
Lennon, Bausman & Fitzgerald

FOOD STYLING
Cindy Syme
Mary Ann Mason

PRODUCTION
Pre-press: Encore Color Group
Printing: Litho Specialties, Inc.

Front cover photograph: *Bifteck au poivre* with Grilled Onion Rounds
Back cover photograph: Swirled Black Pepper Bread with Marinated Tomato Salad

CONTENTS

· · · · · ·

APPETIZERS AND SNACKS

Savory morsels to enjoy before or between meals

BREAD AND PIZZA

Unadorned or tantalizingly topped–the staff of life

SALADS AND SIDES

A miscellany of accompaniments, centerpieces and luncheon treats

SOUPS AND STEWS

A comforting collection of simmering delights

FISH AND SEAFOOD

A maritime mélange from the Caribbean to the Mediterranean to the Pacific

POULTRY

Chicken and turkey star in a variety of international and regional cuisines

PORK

Innovative ideas featuring the "other white meat"

BEEF AND LAMB

Hearty entrées from blue-collar to black tie

DESSERTS

A surprising array of treats you never thought you could make with pepper

INDEX

INTRODUCTION

Pepper is a much used condiment, entering into almost all the culinary preparations; it is an excitant and a stimulant, and its abuse must therefore be avoided.

–from <u>Larousse Gastronomique</u>

When the above-quoted French encyclopedia of food, wine and cookery was published in 1938, its author, Prosper Montagné, was reflecting the tastes of the times. Spice was something to be used sparingly, with prudence and reserve; not thrown about with reckless abandon.

Tastes do change, however; in these days of high-flavor/low-fat cooking, bold tastes are the rule—the more exciting and stimulating, the better. (In fact, spice consumption in the United States has increased by 50 percent in the past decade.) Of the total spice usage nationwide, about a third is devoted to pepper. In 1991, the American Spice Trade Association reported that Americans used over 85.6 million pounds of black pepper, for an average of about 5 ounces per person. That's a staggering amount, considering that one ounce of black pepper will season about 1,440 eggs.

Black pepper is, without a doubt, the world's most popular and important spice. It is used in virtually every cuisine in the world. With a taste that is neither sweet nor savory (usually described as "pungent"), it can be used in both types of food. Its versatility and popularity have earned it the title "The King of Spices," even putting it on a level with salt, one of the basic substances of life. In fact, the words "salt and pepper" have become so firmly entrenched in the lexicon of cooking that many recipes omit them altogether as ingredients, simply assuming their presence. With regard to pepper, at least, that oversight won't happen here.

A HISTORY OF PEPPER

Pepper is the unripe fruit of the *Piper nigrum* vine native to the monsoon forests of the Malabar coast in southwest India, where it was referred to in Sanskrit inscriptions as long as 3,000 years ago.

There are actually two species of pepper: *Piper longum*, or "long pepper," also native to the region, was referred to in Sanskrit as *pippali*, which was the origin of the term "pepper." Its berries, about an inch long, resemble the catkins found in North American birch forests. Long pepper, in fact, was probably the first variety of pepper to reach the Mediterranean. Both varieties were described by the Greek philosopher Theophrastus in the fourth century B.C., and by the Roman historian Pliny in the first century A.D.

The ancient Greeks and Romans both loved pepper in their food, and used it as a form of currency, weighing it out like gold (which it rivaled in price per ounce). In those days, long pepper was more expensive than black pepper, and the Romans imposed a customs duty on it in A.D. 176, exempting the black variety. The ancient world's version of a marketing disaster, this is probably the most important reason for the near-demise of long pepper and the meteoric rise of black pepper.

Black pepper spread from the Roman Empire throughout Europe. When the Visigoths laid siege to Rome in A.D. 408, Alaric demanded gold, silver, and 3,000 pounds of pepper as the ransom. After the Empire fell, the trade routes to India were closed, and pepper was virtually unobtainable anywhere in Europe. During the Crusades, European soldiers campaigning in the Holy Land managed to bring pepper with them. Having been obtained at the expense of Christian blood and transported over a long and perilous route, the spice was predictably costly, and was once again used as currency. A common phrase used in those days to describe someone of little means was "he hath no pepper" (akin to the similar phrase, "not worth his salt").

The use of pepper as legal tender lasted for centuries. In the Middle Ages, peppercorns were used to pay rents, dowries and taxes. Today, in fact, many churches and public lands in Britain are leased for a "peppercorn rent" (a symbolic token). For example, the Ritz Hotel in London leases its garden from the Queen for an annual

Piper nigrum

fee of one peppercorn.

The European taste for pepper and other spices led them to expend a great deal of energy, money and manpower in search of a more direct route to India and the mysterious "spice islands" of the East, culminating in the Spanish monarchy's funding of the 1492 expedition of the famous Genoese adventurer, Christopher Columbus.

Columbus succeeded in finding lands rich in spices, to be sure. Unfortunately, what he believed to be pepper was in fact allspice, which to this day is known in Spanish as *pimienta*, or "pepper." Later Anglicized to "pimento," allspice is known to most of Europe as "Jamaica pepper." Columbus' journey resulted in two other misconceptions which live on today: Because he believed he had found India, the native peoples of the New World were bestowed with the misnomer "Indians." Also, the incendiary fruits of the local *Capsicum* vines, known as *axi* to the Carib people, became known as "peppers" because of their biting heat. (The more proper term for capsicums is *chiles*.)

Six years after Columbus' first voyage, the Portuguese explorer Vasco de Gama changed the course of history when he discovered a way to reach Calcutta by sailing around the southern tip of Africa. Returning to Europe with his ship's hold brimming with pepper, de Gama not only succeeded in greatly lowering the price of pepper, but he almost singlehandedly shifted the world's balance of power from the spice ports of Venice and Genoa to his own Portugal. Subsequent efforts by other explorers would make power centers of Holland, England...and Salem, Massachusetts.

A Salem native named Elihu Yale reached India in 1672 and founded a spice business that would earn him a vast fortune, with which he founded Yale University. Another of the New World's first millionaires, Elias Hasket Derby, also hailed from Salem, and also made his fortune in the pepper business. From 1799 to 1846 millions of dollars worth of *Piper nigrum* was brought to Salem by Yankee skippers who founded America's merchant marine.

Toward the end of the 1800s, the United States ceased to be an active participant in the world spice trade because of increasing incidents of piracy on the high seas. That was to have no real effect on the availability of pepper and other spices, however; the spice market was by then well established, and pepper was to be found on the shelf of every pantry.

GROWING, HARVESTING AND PROCESSING

Pepper is a perennial vine that thrives in tropical climates within 15 degrees of the Equator. The main producers are India, Malaysia (Borneo), Indonesia (Sumatra), and Brazil. Pepper vines are trained to stakes, or to trees grown for shade in coffee plantations, and grow to a height of 15 feet (5 m). The vine takes seven to eight years to reach full maturity, and continues to bear fruit for 15 to 20 years. Each vine produces hundreds of flower spikes, each of which will bear a cluster, or raceme (as with grapes), of about 50 berries.

The berries are harvested over a two- to three-month period in the spring and summer. For black pepper, the berries are picked before they ripen, and are still green. Workers harvest the berries by beating or rubbing the spikes by hand until the berries separate from their stalks. The berries are soaked in water for a week to 10 days, then spread on mats to dry in the tropical sun for another three or four days. This begins the process of fermentation, which enhances the pungency of the peppercorns and makes their skin dry, wrinkled, black, and spicy.

White pepper comes from the same plant as black, but the berries are allowed to ripen fully on the vine, where they change from green to yellow to red. The ripe berries are soaked in water for a few days to soften the skin, which is then rubbed off to expose the grayish-white peppercorn underneath. The peppercorns are then sun-dried for a day or two until they turn a creamy white. White pepper can also be made more cheaply by mechanically removing the skins of black peppercorns. The resulting pepper, called "decorticated white pepper," is sold mostly to food manufacturers.

VARIETIES OF PEPPER AND SIMILAR SPICES

There are different colors of peppercorns (like black and white), different varieties within those colors (as with varieties of red and white wine), and some spices called "pepper" that really aren't pepper at all. In general, pepper has a warm, somewhat woody smell and a pungent taste. White pepper tastes hotter and less "rounded" because of the flavor components that were removed with the skin. As with coffee beans and wine grapes, varieties of peppercorns can have different flavor characteristics that are dependent on climate, soil and growing conditions.

Some individuals and ethnic groups have preferences; for example, cooks in China and Japan seldom use black pepper, but could not do without white pepper. Although most people can't tell the difference between varieties, many chefs like to mix their favorites into a signature blend, sometimes adding one or more similar spices for a unique slant.

Black Peppercorns

Malabar From the birthplace of pepper, on the southwest coast of India. Though the peppercorns are small, they are full-bodied, strong, and aromatic; a favorite of many, and the "original" pepper.

Tellicherry Also from the Malabar coast, but larger and milder, with a taste variously described as "toasty" and "fruity." Often used in salami; considered the best by many for using whole and grinding fresh in a peppermill.

Lampong Grown in the Lampong district of the Indonesian island of Sumatra. Small peppercorns, with a very bold and pungent flavor—even stronger than Malabar.

Sarawak From the northern coast of Borneo, in Malaysia. Small, dark brown peppercorns yield a lighter-colored pepper with a mild, fruity flavor.

Brazilian A relative newcomer in the pepper world; grown on plantations started by the Japanese after World War II. Mellow and mild; often used in blends.

White Peppercorns

Muntok A relative of Lampong Black from an island off the coast of Sumatra, this variety is grown exclusively for making white pepper. Hot, with a slightly musty aroma.

Sarawak Same as the black variety, but processed as white pepper. Mild, usually used in blends.

Brazilian As above.

Green Peppercorns

The immature berries set aside before being processed into black pepper. Sometimes available fresh, but usually packed in brine or freeze-dried.

Brine-packed The most common form. Mildly sour, but not hot. May be used whole or chopped, like capers.

Freeze-dried Usually not found by itself, but rather as an ingredient in multi-colored pepper blends. Milder than any black peppercorns, and expensive.

Pink Peppercorns

Not really pepper at all, but the fruit of *Schinus molle*, a relative of the mountain ash tree from the island of Réunion near Madagascar. These berries, which are the same size as small peppercorns, taste mildly aromatic, rather than pungent. More properly called "pepper rose," they are usually found in multi-colored pepper blends.

Long Pepper

Described here earlier under "A History of Pepper." Botanically named *Piper longum*, this plant is related to *Piper nigrum*, and grows wild from the foothills of the Himalayas to southern India. The two varieties taste much the same, with long pepper being a bit less pungent and having a bit of sweetness. Today, long pepper is generally found only in the Far East and in certain esoteric spice blends from North Africa and Ethiopia.

Cayenne (Red) Pepper

This ferociously hot powder is not a type of pepper at all, but rather a ground chile product, made from small red *Capsicum annuum* and *Capsicum frutescens* peppers grown in Louisiana, Africa, India, Pakistan, China, and Japan. Cayenne peppers got their name from the city of Cayenne in French Guiana, where, oddly enough, they are no longer grown. Sometimes simply called "red pepper," cayenne is used very sparingly in French cuisine as an accent to a cream sauce or mayonnaise, and not sparingly at all in other places, like India, Morocco, and Cajun Louisiana.

Cubeb

A member of the pepper family, *Piper cubeba* is native to Indonesia. Also known as "tailed pepper," cubebs resemble peppercorns with little tails. Their flavor is closer to allspice than to pepper, and they are used mostly in Indonesian cuisine and by the liquor industry to flavor gin.

Szechuan Peppercorns

Also known as *fagara*, anise pepper, or flower pepper, *Xanthoxylum piperitum* is the reddish-brown dried berry of the Chinese prickly ash tree. Used exclusively in Chinese cuisine, it is sometimes roasted and mixed with salt as a table condiment, and is an ingredient in Chinese Five-Spice Powder. Many chefs like to add it to their peppercorn blend in a peppermill. The Japanese version of the same tree yields a similar spice called *sansho*.

Allspice

Mistaken as pepper by Columbus, *Pimenta dioica* is also called "Jamaica pepper." The name "allspice" comes from its flavor, which resembles a peppery combination of cloves, cinnamon and nutmeg. The round dried berries are a bit larger than peppercorns, and may also be added to one's peppercorn blend to give a Caribbean flavor.

Grains of Paradise

Now fallen into obscurity, *Aframomum melegueta* is related to cardamom. Also called "Guinea pepper" or "Melegueta pepper," it has a hot, peppery taste and was once used as a cheap filler or replacement for true pepper when its price was high. Found mainly in West African cuisine, and also as a flavoring for gin.

PEPPER THE WATKINS WAY

One of the finest manufacturers of black pepper in the world is Watkins Incorporated, of Winona, Minnesota. Founded in 1868 by J.R. Watkins, the company began selling black pepper in 1895. Watkins products are not available in supermarkets; the spices, extracts and other food products must be purchased from a Watkins Independent Representative.

Watkins Black Pepper gained a reputation for quality on the farms and prairies of Minnesota, where it was first sold, and the word spread quickly. The company's strict attention to quality and purity earned their product the Grand Prix with Gold Medal at the 1928 Paris International Exposition.

Watkins has always purchased the best peppercorns available on the market. The preferred varieties for processing are Malabar and Lampong, for their superior strength. These top grade peppercorns are always clean and uniform, and are carefully screened for twigs and other fillers before being *granulated*. Many pepper processors grind their pepper to a fine powder, resulting in a product with a lot of pepper dust, or fines, that seem to wind up in the cook's nose as much as in the food. Watkins' exclusive process involves sending the peppercorns through a steel corrugated roller mill which chips each berry into fine particles, to avoid crushing the tiny oil cells. This results in a much more flavorful product.

Watkins Pepper has become so popular that the company released a line of pepper products designed to fit a variety of tastes and cooking styles. They include the famous Granulated Black Pepper and the coarse Cracked Black Pepper, as well as a variety of blends incorporating the company's top-quality herbs and spices. Whole-peppercorn blends for the peppermill are becoming increasingly popular, too, such as Royal Pepper Blend, a mélange of black, white, green and pink peppercorns.

The recipes in this book were developed to showcase the fine flavor of Watkins Pepper in its various forms. Enjoy it, and remember—when you use the King of Spices, use the best.

CAJUN PEANUTS

. . . . .

A spicy accompaniment to your favorite beverage.

2 tsp/10 ml vegetable or peanut oil
2 cups/500 ml cocktail or dry roasted peanuts
1 tbsp/15 ml Watkins Cajun Pepper, more or less to taste

Heat oil in large skillet. Add peanuts and Cajun Pepper; toss to coat. Heat just until warm. Drain on paper toweling.

Makes 2 cups/500 ml, 1 tbsp/15 ml per serving.

NUTRITIONAL INFORMATION PER SERVING: Calories 60, Protein 2 g, Carbohydrates 2 g, Fat 5 g, Sat Fat 1 g, Cholesterol 0 mg, Sodium 50 mg, Dietary Fiber 1 g.

GARLIC PEPPER CHEESE

. . . . .

This can also be placed in an attractive container with the Garlic Peppercorn Blend sprinkled on top.

2 packages (8 oz/227 g each) cream cheese, softened
2¹/₂ tsp/12.5 ml Watkins Italian Seasoning
³/₄ tsp/4 ml Watkins Garlic Powder
³/₄ tsp/4 ml Watkins Onion Powder
2 tbsp/30 ml cracked Watkins Garlic Peppercorn Blend

Combine cream cheese, Italian seasoning and garlic and onion powders; mix well.

Spoon into a cylinder on a sheet of plastic wrap. Roll up tightly in plastic wrap so cylinder holds shape; refrigerate 6 to 8 hours. Remove cheese from refrigerator and peel off plastic wrap. Pat garlic pepper evenly over cheese. Cover and store in the refrigerator. Slice and serve with assorted whole wheat crackers or toasted bread.

Makes 16 servings.

NUTRITIONAL INFORMATION PER SERVING: Calories 100, Protein 2 g, Carbohydrates 1 g, Fat 10 g, Sat Fat 6 g, Cholesterol 31 mg, Sodium 80 mg, Dietary Fiber 0 g.

GOAT CHEESE WITH
ROYAL PEPPER BLEND
· · · · · ·

This pretty and easy appetizer is delicious with toasted whole-grain bread or crackers.

One 5 ¹/₂-oz/156-g log or disc fresh
  goat cheese
1 tbsp/15 ml Watkins Royal Pepper Blend,
  coarsely crushed
2 tsp/10 ml extra-virgin olive oil
Watkins Royal Pepper Blend, for garnish

Bring goat cheese to room temperature and place in a small bowl. Add crushed peppercorns; mix well.

Line 1-cup/227-ml ramekin or bowl with plastic wrap. Transfer cheese mixture into ramekin and pack it down with back of spoon. Unmold onto serving plate. Smooth surface with a heated knife and drizzle with olive oil. Garnish with whole Royal Peppercorns and fresh parsley sprigs. Serve with bread or crackers.

Makes 8 servings.

NUTRITIONAL INFORMATION PER SERVING: Calories 70, Protein 4 g, Carbohydrates 0 g, Fat 6 g, Sat Fat 3 g, Cholesterol 14 mg, Sodium 160 mg, Dietary Fiber 0 g.

SALMON SPREAD
· · · · · ·

Garnish this tasty spread with fresh dill sprigs. Or place in a fish mold that has been lined with plastic wrap.

1 can (15 oz/425 g) red salmon, drained
1 package (8 oz/227 g) cream cheese,
  softened
3 tbsp/45 ml mayonnaise
1¹/₂ tbsp/25 ml Watkins Onion Flakes
³/₄ tsp/4 ml Watkins Sherry Flavor
¹/₂ tsp/2.5 ml Watkins Lemon Pepper
¹/₂ tsp/2.5 ml Watkins Dill Weed

Remove the large bones and dark skin from salmon. Gently mix all ingredients together with a fork. Place in a crock and refrigerate at least 4 hours. Serve with pita bread wedges or assorted whole wheat crackers.

Makes 2¹/₂ cups/625 ml, 1 tbsp/15 ml per serving.

NUTRITIONAL INFORMATION PER SERVING: Calories 40, Protein 3 g, Carbohydrates 0 g, Fat 3 g, Sat Fat 2 g, Cholesterol 13 mg, Sodium 80 mg, Dietary Fiber 0 g.

P E P P E R

BLACK PEPPER GOUGÈRES
· · · · · ·

Pronounced *goo-ZHARE*, these charming snacks, reminiscent of miniature popovers, can be served hot or cold.

1 cup/250 ml grated Gruyère or Swiss cheese
1 cup/250 ml water
5 tbsp/75 ml butter
³/₄ tsp/4 ml Watkins Garlic Salt
¹/₂ tsp/2.5 ml Watkins Black Pepper
1 cup all-purpose flour
5 large eggs, room temperature

Preheat oven to 425°F./220°C. In medium saucepan, bring the water, butter, garlic salt, and pepper to a boil. When butter has melted, remove from heat.

Add flour to butter/water mixture and beat with a spoon until mixture leaves sides of pan clean. Add cheese and beat until incorporated. Beat in 4 eggs, one at a time, until thoroughly absorbed. Beat until mixture is smooth, shiny and firm.

Drop dough by small spoonfuls onto a lightly greased cookie sheet. Beat remaining egg with 1¹/₂ tsp/7.5 ml water, then brush tops of uncooked puffs with egg wash. Bake in upper third of oven for about 20 minutes or until puffs are golden and are doubled in size. Remove from oven and serve.

Makes 36 puffs, 1 per serving.

NUTRITIONAL INFORMATION PER SERVING: Calories 50, Protein 2 g, Carbohydrates 3 g, Fat 3 g, Sat Fat 2 g, Cholesterol 34 mg, Sodium 60 mg, Dietary Fiber 0 g.

CRISPY CHICKEN APPETIZERS

· · · · · ·

Accompany these appetizers with Watkins Country Mill Mustard or prepared Watkins Barbecue Sauce. Or prepare a quick apricot sauce by combining apricot preserves and Watkins Onion Mustard, to taste.

2 cups/500 ml cornflake crumbs, lightly crushed
1 1/2 tsp/7.5 ml Watkins Black Pepper
1 tsp/5 ml Watkins Garlic Salt
3/4 tsp/4 ml Watkins Onion Powder
2 whole chicken breasts, skinned, boned, halved and cut
  crosswise into 1/2-inch/1-cm strips
1/2 cup/125 ml butter, melted

Heat oven to 425°F./220°C. In shallow bowl, combine cornflake crumbs, pepper, garlic salt, and onion powder. Dip chicken pieces in melted butter; roll in cereal mixture, coating evenly. Place on large ungreased baking pan with sides.

Bake at 425°F./220°C. for 10 to 15 minutes or until chicken is no longer pink and coating is crisp. Serve warm.

Makes 30 appetizers, 1 per serving.

NUTRITIONAL INFORMATION PER SERVING: Calories 40, Protein 2 g, Carbohydrates 2 g, Fat 3 g, Sat Fat 2 g, Cholesterol 13 mg, Sodium 90 mg, Dietary Fiber 0 g.

P E P P E R

BUFFALO RIBS
· · · · · ·

A pork version of the famous tavern chicken wings.

2 pounds/1 kg back ribs, cut into 1-rib portions
5 tbsp/75 ml butter, melted
2¹/₂ tbsp/40 ml Watkins Inferno Hot Pepper Sauce
³/₄ cup/180 ml crushed cornflake crumbs
1 to 1¹/₂ tsp/5 to 7.5 ml Watkins Cajun Pepper

In small bowl, mix together butter and Inferno sauce. In shallow plate, mix together cornflake crumbs and Cajun Pepper. Dip ribs in butter mixture and then roll in cornflake mixture. Place ribs an inch apart on an ungreased cookie sheet or shallow pan. Bake at 350°F./180°C. for 45 minutes or until golden brown. Serve with Bleu Cheese Sauce (recipe follows), for dipping, if desired.

Makes 8 servings.

NUTRITIONAL INFORMATION PER SERVING: Calories 100, Protein 2 g, Carbohydrates 3 g, Fat 9 g, Sat Fat 5 g, Cholesterol 26 mg, Sodium 250 mg, Dietary Fiber 0 g.

BLEU CHEESE SAUCE
· · · · · ·

1 cup/250 ml sour cream
1¹/₂ tbsp/25 ml Watkins Pepper Ranch Dip Seasoning
¹/₄ cup/60 ml crumbled bleu cheese

Combine all ingredients and mix well.

Makes 1¹/₄ cups/325 ml, 8 servings.

NUTRITIONAL INFORMATION PER SERVING: Calories 90, Protein 2 g, Carbohydrates 3 g, Fat 8 g, Sat Fat 5 g, Cholesterol 18 mg, Sodium 180 mg, Dietary Fiber 0 g.

CAPONATA

· · · · · ·

This Sicilian classic can be served as a salad, side dish, or relish.

1 pound/454 g eggplant, peeled and cut into
   ¹/₂-inch/1-cm cubes (about 4 cups/1 liter)
Salt
2 tbsp/30 ml olive oil
1 cup/250 ml finely chopped celery
1¹/₂ tsp/7.5 ml Watkins Basil Liquid Spice
1 tsp/5 ml Watkins Oregano Liquid Spice
1 tsp/5 ml Watkins Garlic Liquid Spice
³/₄ cup/180 ml finely chopped onion
8 ounces/227 g fresh mushrooms, cleaned
   and chopped
1 can (14 ¹/₂ oz/411 g) diced tomatoes
   and juice
1 can (8 oz/227 g) tomato sauce
1 tsp/5 ml Watkins Seasoning Salt
1 tsp/5 ml Watkins Italian Pepper
¹/₄ cup/60 ml balsamic vinegar
¹/₃ cup/80 ml chopped pimento-stuffed
   green olives
2 tbsp/30 ml capers (optional)
Italian or French bread, about 2 inches/5 cm
   in diameter, sliced ¹/₂-inch/1-cm thick
   and toasted
Whole wheat crackers
Assorted cut fresh vegetables such as
   carrots, celery, or zucchini

Sprinkle cubed eggplant generously with salt and set in a colander to drain. After about 30 minutes, pat the cubes dry with paper towels and set them aside.

Heat the vegetable oil in a large nonstick skillet; add the celery and cook over medium heat, stirring frequently, for 10 minutes. Add the liquid spices, onion, eggplant and mushrooms; cook about 10 minutes or until the celery and onion are soft. Blend in the tomatoes and juice, tomato sauce, seasoning salt, and Italian Pepper; simmer 10 minutes. Remove from heat and stir in the vinegar, olives, and capers. Adjust seasonings if desired.

Transfer Caponata to a serving bowl and refrigerate until ready to serve. Serve with Italian bread, crackers or vegetable dippers.

Makes 5 cups/1.25 liters, ¹/₄ cup/60 ml per serving.

NUTRITIONAL INFORMATION PER SERVING: Calories 40, Protein 1 g, Carbohydrates 5 g, Fat 3 g, Sat Fat 0 g, Cholesterol 0 mg, Sodium 230 mg, Dietary Fiber 2 g.

P E P P E R

LEMON CHICKEN NUGGETS
· · · · · ·

These tasty nuggets with a Greek flair are so flavorful, they don't even need a dipping sauce.

¹/₂ cup/125 ml all-purpose flour
2 tsp/10 ml Watkins Seasoning Salt
1 tsp/5 ml Watkins Paprika
1 tsp/5 m Watkins Onion Powder
1 tsp/5 ml Watkins Oregano
¹/₂ tsp/2.5 ml Watkins Lemon Pepper
¹/₄ tsp/1.25 ml Watkins Garlic Powder
1 pound/454 g skinless, boneless chicken breasts, cut into
* 1-inch/2.5-cm pieces*
1¹/₂ tbsp/25 ml fresh lemon juice
Vegetable oil

Measure first seven ingredients into a plastic bag; close tightly and shake to blend. Moisten chicken with lemon juice. Let stand 30 minutes. Place chicken chunks, a few at a time, into plastic bag. Shake to coat thoroughly.

Pour oil into heavy saucepan, filling no more than ¹/₃ full. Heat to 375°F./190°C. Carefully add chicken, a few pieces at a time. Fry, turning once, about 2 minutes or until tender. Drain on paper towels.

Makes 8 appetizer servings.

NUTRITIONAL INFORMATION PER SERVING: Calories 90, Protein 14 g, Carbohydrates 7 g, Fat 1 g, Sat Fat 0 g, Cholesterol 33 mg, Sodium 300 mg, Dietary Fiber 0 g.

CRUNCHY LEMON PEPPER NUTS

· · · · · ·

These nuts are not only good for snacking, but also make a
crunchy topping for salads.

1 tbsp/15 ml olive oil
1 tbsp/15 ml soy sauce
2 tsp/10 ml Watkins Lemon Pepper
1 tsp/5 ml lemon juice
2 cups/500 ml unsalted nuts (such as pecan
   or walnut halves, or whole almonds)

In medium bowl, combine the olive oil,
soy sauce, lemon pepper, and lemon juice;

mix well. Add nuts and stir until coated.
Spread nuts in an 8-inch/20-cm square
baking dish. Bake at 325°F./165°C. for 15
minutes or until lightly toasted, stirring
twice. Remove from oven and cool. Can be
stored in refrigerator for up to 1 month.
Bring to room temperature before serving.

Makes 2 cups/500 ml, 1 tbsp/15 ml
per serving.

NUTRITIONAL INFORMATION PER SERVING: Calories 50, Protein 1 g, Carbohydrates 1 g, Fat 5 g, Sat Fat 0 g, Cholesterol 0 mg, Sodium 30 mg, Dietary Fiber 0 g.

LEMON PEPPER OLIVES

· · · · · ·

You will find these appetizers throughout the Mediterranean, from Spanish *tapas*
bars to Greek *tavernas*. Serve them with your favorite cocktail, such as Spanish dry
sherry or Greek *ouzo*, or put them in a decorative jar wrapped with a bow as a gift.

1 jar (10 oz/283 g) pimento-stuffed olives
1 1/2 tsp/7.5 ml Watkins Cracked Black Pepper
1 tsp/5 ml Watkins Garlic Flakes
1/2 tsp/2.5 ml Watkins Oregano
2 lemon slices
3 tbsp/45 ml fresh lemon juice

Drain olives and reserve brine. Combine
seasonings and set aside. In olive jar, layer

1/2 of the olives, 1/2 of the seasoning
mixture, and 1 lemon slice. Repeat
layering. Pour lemon juice over the top
and fill with reserved olive brine. Screw
on lid and shake to combine. Chill at least
48 hours. Store in refrigerator for up to
4 weeks.

Makes 32 appetizer servings.

NUTRITIONAL INFORMATION PER SERVING: Calories 10, Protein 0 g, Carbohydrates 0 g, Fat 1 g, Sat Fat 0 g, Cholesterol 0 mg, Sodium 210 mg, Dietary Fiber 0 g.

LEMON PEPPER AND PARMESAN CRACKERS
· · · · · ·

For a twist on the wine and cheese theme, pair these elegant appetizers with a glass of wine.

1½ cups/375 ml finely grated Parmesan cheese
  (about 4 oz/113 g)
¾ cup/180 ml all-purpose flour
1 tsp/5 ml Watkins Lemon Pepper
½ stick (¼ cup/60 ml) cold unsalted butter, cut into bits
5 tsp/25 ml water
1 tsp/5 ml fresh lemon juice
Watkins Lemon Pepper, if desired

In medium bowl, combine cheese, flour, and lemon pepper. Cut in butter with a pastry blender until mixture resembles coarse crumbs. Make a well in center and add water and lemon juice. Combine with a fork until mixture forms a dough.

On work surface, knead dough until combined; transfer to a sheet of wax paper. Form dough into 8-x1-inch/20-x2.5-cm log. Wrap in waxed paper and chill for at least one hour or until firm enough to slice.

Preheat oven to 375°F./190°C. Cut the dough into ¼-inch/.5-cm-thick slices. Arrange slices 1 inch/2.5 cm apart on baking sheets. Bake in batches, in the middle of the oven for 10 to 12 minutes or until edges are golden. Carefully transfer crackers to wire rack to cool. Sprinkle with additional pepper, if desired.

Makes 36 crackers, 1 per serving.

NUTRITIONAL INFORMATION PER SERVING: Calories 20, Protein 0 g, Carbohydrates 2 g, Fat 1 g, Sat Fat 1 g, Cholesterol 4 mg, Sodium 5 mg, Dietary Fiber 0 g.

WHITE BEAN AND BREAD CRUMB SKORDALIA
· · · · · ·

This garlicky Greek spread is commonly made with a lot of olive oil, but this recipe uses only a small amount for flavoring.

Five 1-inch/2.5-cm thick slices day-old
    French or Italian bread, crust removed
    and cut into chunks
1¹/₂ cups/375 ml canned, drained and rinsed
    cannellini or other white beans
4 tsp/20 ml lemon juice
³/₄ tsp/4 ml Watkins Black Pepper
1 tsp/5 ml Watkins Garlic Liquid Spice
1 tsp/5 ml extra-virgin olive oil
¹/₄ cup/60 ml water

Place bread chunks in a food processor or blender and process into coarse crumbs. Add beans, lemon juice, and black pepper; process until smooth. With motor running, pour in liquid spice, olive oil and water. Let stand for at least 30 minutes to allow flavors to blend. Add more water if mixture is too stiff. Garnish with lemon strips and fresh parsley. Serve with *crostini* (recipe follows).

CROSTINI
· · · · · ·

2 tsp/10 ml olive oil
¹/₂ tsp/2.5 ml Watkins Oregano Liquid Spice
¹/₂ tsp/2.5 ml Watkins Garlic Liquid Spice
20 ¹/₄-inch/0.5-cm thick slices French or
    Italian bread

Combine olive oil and liquid spices. Brush on both sides of bread and place on baking sheet. Bake at 350°F./180°C. for 10 minutes or until lightly toasted.

Makes 10 servings.

NUTRITIONAL INFORMATION PER SERVING: Calories 210, Protein 7 g, Carbohydrates 34 g, Fat 5 g, Sat Fat 1 g, Cholesterol 0 mg, Sodium 300 mg, Dietary Fiber 4 g.

SWIRLED BLACK PEPPER BREAD
· · · · · ·

This tasty bread is not only an excellent accompaniment to salads, soups and stews, but is also a great sandwich bread.

1 package (16 oz/454 g) hot roll mix
³/₄ tsp/4 ml Watkins Basil
¹/₄ tsp/1.2 ml Watkins Garlic Powder
¹/₄ tsp/1.2 ml Watkins Onion Powder
2 tbsp/30 ml butter, softened
¹/₂ cup/125 ml finely grated Parmesan cheese
1 tsp/5 ml Watkins Black Pepper
Melted butter

Prepare hot roll mix dough according to package directions for bread, adding the basil and garlic and onion powders to dry mix. Let rest as directed for 5 minutes.

On a lightly-floured surface, roll dough into an 18-x9-inch/ 46-x23-cm rectangle. Spread dough with butter and sprinkle with cheese and pepper. Roll tightly, jelly-roll fashion, starting from a short side. Pinch edges and ends to seal. Place in a greased 9-x5-inch/23-x13-cm loaf pan. Cover with a clean towel and let rise 15 to 20 minutes. Bake at 350°F./180°C. for 35 to 40 minutes or until loaf sounds hollow when lightly tapped. Remove from pan and brush with melted butter. Let cool on wire rack.

Makes 1 loaf, 10 servings.

NUTRITIONAL INFORMATION PER SERVING: Calories 170, Protein 6 g, Carbohydrates 29 g, Fat 5 g, Sat Fat 2 g, Cholesterol 9 mg, Sodium 340 mg, Dietary Fiber 2 g.

BLACK PEPPER AND CHEDDAR BREADSTICKS

· · · · · ·

These chewy breadsticks make a wonderful accompaniment with
Italian dishes and salads.

1 package (14 oz/397 g) Watkins Pizza Crust Mix
2 tsp/10 ml Watkins Black Pepper
1 cup/250 ml finely shredded sharp Cheddar cheese
1/4 cup/60 ml thinly sliced green onion
Approx. 1 cup/250 ml warm water (110°F./43°C.)
1 egg white beaten with 1 tsp/5 ml water
Watkins Garlic and Chives Seasoning or kosher salt

In medium bowl, combine first four ingredients; add enough
water to form a smooth dough. Knead for 5 minutes. Place
in a greased bowl; cover and let stand in warm area for 15
minutes. Break off dough into 12 pieces. Roll each piece
into a rope about 12 inches/30 cm long, twisting if desired.
Place on greased cookie sheet. Brush with egg white mixture
and sprinkle with Garlic and Chives Seasoning or salt. Bake
at 400°F./205°C. for 15 minutes or until golden brown. Let
stand a few minutes before serving.

Makes 12 breadsticks, 1 per serving.

NUTRITIONAL INFORMATION PER SERVING: Calories 70, Protein 4 g, Carbohydrates 7 g, Fat 3 g, Sat Fat 2 g,
Cholesterol 10 mg, Sodium 70 mg, Dietary Fiber 0 g.

HEARTY BLACK PEPPER CORN BREAD
· · · · · ·

Serve this dense, hearty loaf with chili, stew or soup.

1¹/₂ cups/375 ml yellow cornmeal, divided
1¹/₂ tsp/7.5 ml Watkins Black Pepper
1 tsp/5 ml Watkins Seasoning Salt
1 tsp/5 ml Watkins Onion Powder
1 cup/250 ml boiling water
1 package quick-rising yeast
1 tsp/5 ml white sugar
1/4 cup/60 ml hot water
   (125°-135°F./50°-55°C.)
1 tbsp/15 ml olive oil
1 to 2 cups/250 to 500 ml bread flour,
   divided

Mix 1 cup/250 ml of the cornmeal, pepper, seasoning salt, and onion powder with the boiling water until smooth. Let mixture cool to 120°F./50°C. about 10 minutes. Mix in yeast, sugar, the ¹/₄ cup/60 ml hot water, and oil. Add 1 cup/250 ml of the bread flour and mix until smooth and elastic, about 5 minutes. Cover bowl with a damp cloth and let rise in warm draft-free area until puffy, about 45 minutes.

Grease a 9-inch/23-cm glass pie plate with vegetable oil. Knead enough of the remaining bread flour into dough to make it nonsticky. Knead on floured surface until smooth and elastic, about 5 minutes. Knead into a ball. Place in pan and flatten to fill bottom of pan. Cover with a towel and let rise in a warm place until doubled, about 50 minutes.

Score top of bread in a tic-tac-toe pattern. Bake at 350°F./180°C. for 35 to 45 minutes or until bread is light brown and top sounds hollow when tapped. Remove from pan and serve warm or cool on wire rack.

Makes 1 loaf, 10 servings.

NUTRITIONAL INFORMATION PER SERVING: Calories 180, Protein 5 g, Carbohydrates 36 g, Fat 2 g, Sat Fat 0 g, Cholesterol 0 mg, Sodium 110 mg, Dietary Fiber 3 g.

PEPPERED BUTTERMILK BISCUITS WITH HONEY BUTTER
· · · · · ·

Sweet honey butter enhances the spiceness of these light and flaky biscuits.

$1^3/_4$ cups plus 2 tbsp/470 ml all-purpose flour
1 tbsp/15 ml Watkins Baking Powder
1 tsp/5 ml Watkins Black Pepper
$^1/_2$ tsp/2.5 ml Watkins Seasoning Salt
3 tbsp/45 ml chilled unsalted butter
$2^1/_2$ tbsp/40 ml solid vegetable shortening
$^3/_4$ cup/180 ml chilled buttermilk

Preheat oven to 450°F./235°C. Combine first four ingredients in medium bowl. Add butter and shortening and rub with fingertips until coarse crumbs form. Mix in buttermilk. Turn dough out onto floured work surface; knead gently until combined, about 20 seconds. Roll out dough to a thickness of $^1/_2$-inch/1-cm. Cut out biscuits using a 2-inch/5-cm cookie cutter. Gather scraps, reroll and cut out more biscuits. Place on ungreased baking sheet, spacing evenly. Bake 15 minutes or until golden brown. Serve warm with Honey Butter (recipe follows).

Makes 12 biscuits, 1 per serving.

NUTRITIONAL INFORMATION PER SERVING: Calories 120, Protein 2 g, Carbohydrates 15 g, Fat 6 g, Sat Fat 3 g, Cholesterol 8 mg, Sodium 140 mg, Dietary Fiber 1 g.

HONEY BUTTER
· · · · · ·

$^1/_2$ cup/125 ml unsalted butter
2 tbsp/30 ml honey

Combine and mix thoroughly.

Makes $^1/_2$ cup/125 ml, 1 tsp/5 ml per serving.

NUTRITIONAL INFORMATION PER SERVING: Calories 40, Protein 0 g, Carbohydrates 1 g, Fat 4 g, Sat Fat 2 g, Cholesterol 10 mg, Sodium 1 mg, Dietary Fiber 0 g.

ONION-PEPPER BISCUITS
. . . . . .

These flavorful biscuits take only minutes to make.

1 can (10 oz/283 g) refrigerated
  flaky biscuits
1¹/₂ tbsp/25 ml Watkins Onion Flakes
  rehydrated with 1¹/₂ tbsp/25 ml water
1 tbsp/15 ml butter
¹/₂ tsp/2.5 ml Watkins Cracked Black Pepper

Place biscuits on ungreased baking sheet. Sauté onion flakes in butter. Spoon mixture over biscuits; sprinkle with pepper and press down lightly. Bake at 375°F./190°C. for 15 to 20 minutes.

Makes 10 biscuits, 1 per serving.

NUTRITIONAL INFORMATION PER SERVING: Calories 100, Protein 2 g, Carbohydrates 14 g, Fat 4 g, Sat Fat 2 g, Cholesterol 5 mg, Sodium 360 mg, Dietary Fiber 0 g.

CHILI-PEPPER CORN MUFFINS
. . . . . .

An excellent accompaniment to chili and stews.

1¹/₂ cups/375 ml all-purpose flour
¹/₂ cup/125 ml yellow cornmeal
2 tsp/10 ml Watkins Baking Powder
1 tsp/5 ml Watkins Chili Powder
¹/₂ tsp/2.5 ml Watkins Cracked Black Pepper
¹/₂ tsp/2.5 ml Watkins Garlic Salt
1¹/₂ cups/375 ml buttermilk
2 large eggs, beaten
2 tbsp/30 ml olive oil
2 tbsp/30 ml melted unsalted butter, cooled

Preheat oven to 425°F./200°C. Grease eight 2¹/₂-inch/6-cm muffin cups; set aside. In medium bowl, combine flour and next five ingredients; mix well. In another bowl, combine buttermilk and remaining three ingredients; mix well. Make a well in center of flour mixture; pour in liquid mixture and stir just until blended. Pour into muffin cups. Bake for 12 to 15 minutes or until muffins test done. Serve warm.

Makes 8 servings.

NUTRITIONAL INFORMATION PER SERVING: Calories 212, Protein 6 g, Carbohydrates 27 g, Fat 8 g, Sat Fat 3 g, Cholesterol 63 mg, Sodium 240 mg, Dietary Fiber 1 g.

GARLIC-PEPPER PULL-APARTS

. . . . . .

These make a wonderful accompaniment to any dish and take only minutes to prepare.

1 package (8 oz/227 g) cream cheese, softened
1¹/₂ tsp/7.5 ml finely cracked Watkins Garlic Peppercorn Blend
1 tsp/5 ml Watkins Basil
1 tsp/5 ml Watkins Parsley
1 can (8 oz/227 g) refrigerated crescent dinner roll dough

In small bowl, combine cream cheese, Garlic Peppercorn Blend, basil, and parsley; set aside. Unroll dough into two rectangles. Place side by side and press perforations to seal. You should end up with an 8-x12-inch/20-x30-cm rectangle. Spread cream cheese mixture evenly over dough. Starting with long end, roll up jelly-roll fashion. Cut into 12 equal slices. Place slices in a greased bundt/tube pan, cut side down. Bake at 375°F./190°C. for 20 to 25 minutes or until golden brown. Remove from oven and invert onto serving plate. Serve hot.

Makes 6 servings.

NUTRITIONAL INFORMATION PER SERVING: Calories 270, Protein 5 g, Carbohydrates 16 g, Fat 21 g, Sat Fat 8 g, Cholesterol 45 mg, Sodium 420 mg, Dietary Fiber 0 g.

SAGE-PEPPER POPOVERS

· · · · ·

The combination of eggs and steam make popovers pop. Serve these tasty popovers piping hot along with the savory butter.

3 eggs
1 cup/250 ml milk, room temperature
3 tbsp/45 ml butter, melted
1 cup/250 ml all-purpose flour
¹/₂ tsp/2.5 ml Watkins Sage
¹/₂ tsp/2.5 ml Watkins Seasoning Salt
¹/₄ tsp/1.2 ml Watkins Black Pepper

Generously grease nine 3-inch/8-cm muffin-pan cups; set aside. With electric mixer at low speed, beat eggs slightly; beat in milk and melted butter. Gradually beat in flour and seasonings. Divide batter among the prepared muffin cups. Bake at 375°F./190°C. for 40 minutes, then remove from oven. Quickly cut a slit in side of each to let steam escape. Return to oven for 10 minutes or until tops are firm, crisp, and brown. Remove from pan. Serve piping hot with Sage-Pepper Butter (recipe follows).

Makes 9 popovers, 1 per serving.

NUTRITIONAL INFORMATION PER SERVING: Calories 130, Protein 4 g, Carbohydrates 12 g, Fat 6 g, Sat Fat 4 g, Cholesterol 85 mg, Sodium 124 mg, Dietary Fiber 0 g.

SAGE-PEPPER BUTTER

· · · · ·

¹/₂ cup/250 ml butter, softened
¹/₂ tsp/2.5 ml Watkins Sage
¹/₄ tsp/1.2 ml Watkins Black Pepper

Combine all ingredients and mix until smooth. Keep refrigerated until ready to use.

Makes ¹/₂ cup/125 ml, 1 tsp/5 ml per serving.

NUTRITIONAL INFORMATION PER SERVING: Calories 30, Protein 0 g, Carbohydrates 0 g, Fat 4 g, Sat Fat 2 g, Cholesterol 10 mg, Sodium 30 mg, Dietary Fiber 0 g.

GREEK PIZZA
· · · · · ·

A Mediterranean favorite seasoned with garlic, basil, oregano, and lemon pepper.
The Greek olives really make this pizza; however, if you can't find them, feel free
to substitute regular black olives.

1¹/₂ tsp/7.5 ml Watkins Garlic Liquid Spice
2 cups/500 ml chopped onion
2 packages (10 oz/280 g each) frozen spinach, thawed and drained
1 tbsp/45 ml fresh lemon juice
1 tbsp/45 ml Watkins Basil
2 tsp/10 ml Watkins Oregano
1 tsp/5 ml Watkins Lemon Pepper
Salt, to taste

Over medium heat, sauté the onion and spinach in the Liquid Spice
until all moisture is evaporated. Add remaining ingredients and
cool slightly.

Prepare 1 package (14 oz/396 g) Watkins pizza crust mix per package
directions, adding 2 tsp/10 ml Watkins Oregano to crust.

2 medium tomatoes, thinly sliced
¹/₂ cup/125 ml dry bread crumbs
¹/₂ tsp/2.5 ml Watkins Oregano
1¹/₂ cups/375 ml crumbled feta cheese
8 ounces/227 g shredded mozzarella cheese
Chopped Greek (kalamata) olives

To make pizza, place spinach mixture on prepared dough. Combine
bread crumbs and oregano, dip in slices of tomato and place on top of
spinach. Top with feta and mozzarella cheeses and olives. Bake at
400°F./205°C. for 25 to 30 minutes or until crust is golden brown.

Makes 6 servings.

NUTRITIONAL INFORMATION PER SERVING: Calories 290, Protein 20 g, Carbohydrates 21 g, Fat 15 g, Sat Fat 9 g, Cholesterol 45 mg,
Sodium 670 mg, Dietary Fiber 5 g.

GARLIC PEPPER CHICKEN PIZZA

· · · · · ·

A gourmet pizza better than those served in trendy restaurants.

1 package (14 oz/396 g) Watkins Pizza
   Crust Mix
$^{1}/_{2}$ tsp/2.5 ml coarsely crushed Watkins
   Garlic Peppercorn Blend
12 ounces/340 g skinless, boneless chicken
   breasts, cut into $^{1}/_{2}$ -inch/1-cm pieces
$^{1}/_{2}$ cup/125 ml chopped red onion, divided
2 tbsp/30 ml white wine vinegar
2 tbsp/30 ml water
2 tsp/10 ml Watkins Chicken Soup Base
$1^{1}/_{2}$ tsp./7.5 ml coarsely crushed Watkins
   Garlic Peppercorn Blend
1 tsp/5 ml Watkins Garlic Liquid Spice
1 tbsp/15 ml vegetable oil
1 tbsp/15 ml cornstarch
1 tbsp/15 ml water
$1^{1}/_{2}$ cups/375 ml (6 oz/170 g) shredded
   mozzarella cheese
$^{1}/_{3}$ cup/80 ml chopped green pepper
2 tbsp/30 ml sliced almonds

Prepare pizza crust dough according to package directions, adding $^{1}/_{2}$ tsp/2.5 ml crushed garlic pepper to dry mix.

While pizza is rising in oven, combine chicken, $^{1}/_{4}$ cup/60 ml red onion, and next five ingredients; stir to coat. Let stand 10 minutes. Heat the vegetable oil in a large skillet; add chicken pieces. Cook and stir until no longer pink, about 3 minutes.

Stir cornstarch and water together and stir into chicken mixture. Cook and stir until thickened and bubbly. Spoon evenly atop prepared pizza crust. Sprinkle with cheese, green pepper and remaining $^{1}/_{4}$ cup/60 ml onion. Bake at 400°F./205°C. for 12 minutes. Sprinkle with almonds and bake 2 minutes longer or until crust is golden brown.

Makes 8 servings.

NUTRITIONAL INFORMATION PER SERVING: Calories 190, Protein 18 g, Carbohydrates 13 g, Fat 8 g, Sat Fat 3 g, Cholesterol 36 mg, Sodium 220 mg, Dietary Fiber 0 g.

PEPPER

ONION AND GOAT CHEESE PIZZA
· · · · · ·

Sweet onions and savory goat cheese top this tasty pizza. The chopped walnuts add a delightful crunch.

1 package (14 oz/396 g) Watkins Pizza Crust Mix
1 tsp/5 ml Watkins Cracked Black Pepper
2 large onions, thinly sliced (about 4 cups/1 liter)
1 tbsp/15 ml unsalted butter
1 tbsp/15 ml olive oil
1 tsp/5 ml Watkins Garlic Liquid Spice
1 Watkins Bay Leaf
3 tbsp/45 ml white wine vinegar
Salt and Watkins Black Pepper, to taste
12 ounces/340 g goat cheese, crumbled
¹/₃ cup/80 ml chopped walnuts, optional
Watkins Oregano or Rosemary, if desired

Prepare pizza crust dough according to package directions, adding the cracked pepper to dry mix. While dough is rising in oven, sauté onions in a mixture of butter, olive oil, Liquid Spice, and bay leaf until onions are very soft. Add the white wine vinegar and cook until vinegar evaporates; remove bay leaf.

Prepare pizza by covering pizza dough with the goat cheese, then topping with walnuts and onions. If desired, sprinkle with a little oregano or rosemary to taste. Bake at 400°F./205°C. for 20 to 25 minutes or until golden brown.

Makes 6 servings.

NUTRITIONAL INFORMATION PER SERVING: Calories 350, Protein 15 g, Carbohydrates 21 g, Fat 23 g, Sat Fat 11 g, Cholesterol 45 mg, Sodium 495 mg, Dietary Fiber 1.6 g.

SOUTH PACIFIC SHRIMP BOATS
· · · · · ·

This low-calorie dish makes an attractive luncheon presentation.

1 medium pineapple
1 pound/454 g cleaned and cooked medium shrimp
4 ounces/113 g snow peas (fresh or frozen)
1 can (11 oz/318 g) mandarin oranges, drain and reserve juice
^{1}/$_2$ cup sliced celery
^{1}/$_2$ cup chopped onion
1 tbsp/15 ml vegetable oil
1 tbsp/15 ml white wine vinegar
2 tsp/10 ml Watkins Minced Green Onion
1 tsp/5 ml Watkins Parisienne Mustard
^{1}/$_2$ tsp/2.5 ml Watkins Garlic Powder
^{1}/$_2$ tsp/2.5 ml Watkins Lemon Pepper
^{1}/$_4$ tsp/1.2 ml Watkins Celery Seed

Cut pineapple in half lengthwise; cut fruit from shell and into chunks, keeping shell intact. In medium bowl, combine pineapple chunks, shrimp, snow peas, celery, and onion. In small bowl, combine ^{1}/$_2$ cup/125 ml of the reserved orange juice, oil, and remaining ingredients; mix well. Pour over shrimp mixture and toss to coat. Spoon mixture into pineapple shells and chill. To serve, cut each shell half into thirds.

Makes 6 servings.

NUTRITIONAL INFORMATION PER SERVING: Calories 170, Protein 17 g, Carbohydrates 19 g, Fat 3 g, Sat Fat 0 g, Cholesterol 150 mg, Sodium 210 mg, Dietary Fiber 3 g.

ROAST BEEF AND BROCCOLI SALAD

· · · · · ·

Bring this distinctive salad to your next block party or potluck.

7 cups/1.75 liters coarsely chopped fresh broccoli
1 red or yellow bell pepper, cut into thin strips
$^1/_2$ cup/125 ml coarsely chopped onion
$^3/_4$ pound/340 g deli-style roast beef cut into thin strips
  (leftover roast beef can also be substituted)
$^1/_4$ cup/60 ml white wine vinegar
1 tbsp/15 ml water
1 tbsp/15 ml vegetable oil
$1^1/_2$ tsp/7.5 ml soy sauce
1 tsp/5 ml ground Watkins Garlic Peppercorn Blend
$^1/_2$ tsp/2.5 ml Watkins Onion Powder
$^1/_4$ tsp/1.2 ml Watkins Ginger
Lettuce leaves

Steam broccoli or cook in a small amount of boiling water
for 5 minutes or until crisp-tender. Drain and chill. Combine
broccoli, red pepper, onion, and roast beef; set aside.
Combine vinegar and next six ingredients. Pour over
broccoli mixture; toss gently. Cover and chill 2 hours,
stirring occasionally. To serve, place lettuce on serving
platter or individual salad plates and mound salad on top.

Makes 8 servings.

NUTRITIONAL INFORMATION PER SERVING: Calories 120, Protein 15 g, Carbohydrates 9 g, Fat 4 g, Sat Fat 1 g,
Cholesterol 18 mg, Sodium 700 mg, Dietary Fiber 3 g.

P E P P E R

SWEET AND SOUR FRUIT SALAD
· · · · · ·

The touch of lemon pepper adds a delightful zing to this tangy fruit salad.

2 cups/500 ml coarsely chopped apple
(about 2 medium)
2 cans (6¹/₂ oz/184 g each) pineapple
tidbits in own juice, drained
¹/₄ cup/60 ml cider vinegar
1 tbsp/15 ml honey
1 tsp/5 ml Watkins Cole Slaw Seasoning
1 tsp/5 ml Watkins Onion Flakes
¹/₄ tsp/1.2 ml Watkins Lemon Pepper
Lettuce leaves

Combine all ingredients except lettuce in medium bowl; toss to mix. Cover and chill until ready to serve. To serve, place lettuce on individual serving plates and mound fruit salad on top.

Makes 6 servings.

NUTRITIONAL INFORMATION PER SERVING: Calories 50, Protein 0 g, Carbohydrates 13 g, Fat 0 g, Sat Fat 0 g, Cholesterol 0 mg, Sodium 70 mg, Dietary Fiber 1 g.

MARINATED TOMATO SALAD
· · · · · ·

Marinated salads are an integral part of Mediterranean cuisine. In this classic, the onions are not strong, having been softened and mellowed by the vinaigrette. Serve this refreshing salad with crusty French bread to soak up the delicious juices.

12 ripe Italian plum tomatoes
1 red onion, halved and thinly sliced
¹/₄ cup/60 ml red wine vinegar
1 tbsp/15 ml balsamic vinegar
1 tbsp/15 ml extra virgin olive oil
1 tbsp/15 ml Watkins Basil Liquid Spice
¹/₄ tsp/1.2 ml Watkins Garlic Liquid Spice
¹/₄ tsp/1.2 ml Watkins Black Pepper
Salt, to taste
Lettuce leaves

To prepare tomatoes, slice in half lengthwise,

core, and cut into thirds or quarters (depending on how large each tomato is). In large salad bowl, combine all ingredients except lettuce. Toss gently until mixed. Cover and let stand at room temperature for one hour. (If preparing in advance, store covered in the refrigerator but let come back to room temperature before serving.) Serve over a bed of lettuce. Delicious with grilled fish or chicken.

Makes 6 servings.

NUTRITIONAL INFORMATION PER SERVING: Calories 70, Protein 1 g, Carbohydrates 8 g, Fat 5 g, Sat Fat 1 g, Cholesterol 0 mg, Sodium 8 mg, Dietary Fiber 2 g.

STEAK AND POTATO SALAD
. . . . . .

Accompany this hearty dinner salad with hot rolls and fresh fruit.

1 cup/250 ml olive oil
$^1/_4$ cup/60 ml lemon juice
$^1/_3$ cup/80 ml soy sauce
1 tbsp/15 ml Watkins Garlic Powder
1$^1/_2$ tsp/7.5 ml Watkins Celery Seed
1$^1/_2$ tsp/7.5 ml Watkins Black Pepper, more if desired
4 beef top sirloin steaks (about 4 oz/113 g each)
$^1/_4$ cup/60 ml butter
20 oz/567 g small new potatoes, parboiled and drained
$^1/_2$ cup/125 ml chopped onion
4 cups/1 liter assorted torn mixed greens
Cherry tomato halves or pimento strips, for garnish

Combine first six ingredients; reserve $^1/_3$ cup/80 ml
vinaigrette and pour remainder over steaks. Cover and
refrigerate 2 to 6 hours.

Quarter potatoes. Melt butter in skillet. Sauté potatoes
along with onions until potatoes are browned and cooked
through; keep warm. Grill or broil steak to desired doneness;
slice thinly across the grain.

To serve, divide greens on individual serving plates. Top
with potato mixture then steak. Drizzle dressing evenly over
all. Garnish as desired.

Makes 4 servings.

NUTRITIONAL INFORMATION PER SERVING: Calories 720, Protein 40 g, Carbohydrates 45 g, Fat 44 g, Sat Fat 14 g,
Cholesterol 118 mg, Sodium 1550 mg, Dietary Fiber 5 g.

GRILLED ONION ROUNDS

· · · · · ·

A tasty accompaniment to grilled steak or hamburgers.

3 tbsp/45 ml canola oil
1 tsp/5 ml Watkins Seasoning Salt
1 tsp/5 ml Watkins Barbecue Spice
1/4 tsp/1.2 ml Watkins Grill Seasoning
1/4 tsp/1.2 ml Watkins Cracked Black Pepper
3 large sweet onions

Combine first five ingredients; mix well and set aside. Peel onions and cut into 1/2-inch/1-cm slices; do not break apart. Grill 6 inches from coals; 10 minutes on each side or until tender and brown, brushing often with oil/spice mixture.

Makes 8 servings.

NUTRITIONAL INFORMATION PER SERVING: Calories 60, Protein 0 g, Carbohydrates 3 g, Fat 5 g, Sat Fat 0 g, Cholesterol 0 mg, Sodium 170 mg, Dietary Fiber 1 g.

RED POTATO AND ONION BAKE

· · · · · ·

The onions in this dish become caramelized, bringing out their natural sugars; the resulting sweetness contributes to this distinctive flavor combination.

2 pounds/908 g large red potatoes
2 medium-sized red onions
  (about 6 oz/170 g)
2 tbsp/30 ml olive oil
2 tsp/10 ml Watkins Seasoning Salt
1 tsp/5 ml Watkins Black Pepper
1 tsp/5 ml Watkins Thyme

Preheat oven to 425°F./220°C. Scrub

potatoes and cut each into eighths. Halve onions and cut into thick slices. In large roasting pan, toss potatoes and onions with oil. Sprinkle with remaining ingredients and toss again. Roast vegetables, uncovered, 45 minutes, turning once or twice until golden in color and fork-tender. Serve warm.

Makes 6 servings.

NUTRITIONAL INFORMATION PER SERVING: Calories 220, Protein 4 g, Carbohydrates 41 g, Fat 5 g, Sat Fat 1 g, Cholesterol 0 mg, Sodium 360 mg, Dietary Fiber 4 g.

P E P P E R

ORIENTAL CHICKEN SALAD
· · · · · ·

An unique flavor combination is highlighted by crunchy
water chestnuts and snow peas.

1 cup/250 ml uncooked macaroni, small
    twists or bow ties
1¹/₂ tsp/7.5 ml Watkins Chicken Soup Base
3 cups/750 ml chopped cooked chicken
³/₄ cup/180 ml sliced chopped onion
³/₄ cup/180 ml thinly sliced celery
1 can (8 oz/227 g) sliced water chestnuts,
    drained
1 jar (2 oz/57 g) sliced pimento, drained
³/₄ cup/180 ml mayonnaise
1¹/₂ tbsp/25 ml soy sauce
2 tsp/10 ml Watkins Ginger Garlic
    Liquid Spice
³/₄ tsp/4 ml Watkins Black Pepper
3 cups/750 ml fresh snow peas, blanched or
    2 packages (10 oz/283 g each) frozen snow
    peas, thawed
¹/₂ cup/125 ml slivered, toasted almonds

Cook macaroni according to package
directions, substituting the chicken soup
base for salt; drain and rinse with cold
water. Combine macaroni, chicken, onion,
celery, water chestnuts, and pimento; toss
well. Combine mayonnaise and next three
ingredients; mix well. Fold into chicken
mixture. Cover and chill at least 2 hours.
To serve, divide snow peas among six
individual serving plates in a spoke or petal
fashion. Mound chicken in center; sprinkle
with almonds.

Makes 6 servings.

NUTRITIONAL INFORMATION PER SERVING: Calories 540, Protein 28 g, Carbohydrates 29 g, Fat 35 g, Sat Fat 5 g, Cholesterol 79 mg, Sodium 560 mg, Dietary Fiber 6 g.

HONEY MUSTARD CABBAGE SLAW
· · · · · ·

This tangy vegetable and fruit slaw is sure to become one of your favorites.

1/4 cup/60 ml cider vinegar
1/4 cup/60 ml Watkins Country Mill Coarse Ground Mustard
2 tbsp/30 ml brown sugar
1 tbsp/15 ml Watkins Cole Slaw Seasoning
1 tsp/5 ml Watkins Black Pepper
1/2 cup/125 ml mayonnaise
1/2 cup/125 ml sour cream
3 cups/750 ml shredded green cabbage
3 cups/750 ml shredded red cabbage
1/2 cup/125 ml chopped green onion
1 cup/250 ml chopped Red Delicious apple
1/2 cup/125 ml dark raisins, optional

In large bowl, whisk together the first seven ingredients until smooth. Add both cabbages, green onion, apples and raisins; toss to coat. Cover and refrigerate at least 3 hours.

Makes 8 servings.

NUTRITIONAL INFORMATION PER SERVING: Calories 220, Protein 2 g, Carbohydrates 22 g, Fat 15 g, Sat Fat 4 g, Cholesterol 15 mg, Sodium 410 mg, Dietary Fiber 2 g.

POTATO PANCAKES WITH
SPICED APPLESAUCE
. . . . . .

3 large potatoes (about 2 pounds/908 g)
2 eggs
2 tbsp/30 ml all-purpose flour
2 tsp/10 ml Watkins Onion Flakes
1/2 tsp Watkins Black Pepper
1/2 tsp salt
Vegetable oil for frying
1 jar (16 oz/454 g) chunky applesauce
1/2 tsp Watkins Cinnamon
Sour cream, optional

Wash and peel potatoes. Grate coarsely into a large bowl filled with ice water. Let stand 15 minutes. In medium bowl, beat eggs with a whisk. Add flour, onion flakes, pepper, and salt; mix well.

Drain potatoes well and pat dry with a clean dish towel. Measure out about 4 cups/1 liter of potatoes. Add to egg mixture; mix well. In large heavy skillet or electric fry pan, slowly heat 1/8-inch/0.3-cm oil until very hot (not smoking). For each pancake, drop about 1/4 cup/60 ml potato mixture into oil. Do not crowd. With spatula, flatten to make pancakes about 4 inches/10 cm in diameter. Fry 2 to 3 minutes on each side, or until golden and crisp. Drain well on paper towels; keep warm.

Combine applesauce and cinnamon in small saucepan; mix well. Heat thoroughly. Serve warm applesauce over potato pancakes. Top with a dollop of sour cream, if desired.

Makes 12 pancakes, 6 servings.

NUTRITIONAL INFORMATION PER SERVING: Calories 240, Protein 5 g, Carbohydrates 43 g, Fat 6 g, Sat Fat 1 g, Cholesterol 71 mg, Sodium 210 mg, Dietary Fiber 4 g.

MARITIME CHOWDER
· · · · · ·

Chowder is a thick, chunky soup. The term "chowder" comes from the French *chaudière*, meaning "boiler." Fishermen cooked their food fresh from the sea in these large kettles.

$^1/_2$ cup/125 ml chopped green onion
$^1/_2$ cup/125 ml chopped celery
1 tbsp/15 ml Watkins Onion Liquid Spice
2 cups/500 ml bottled clam juice, or water,
   or combination of the two
2 cups/500 ml peeled diced potatoes
$^1/_3$ cup/80 ml Watkins Cream Soup Base
$^3/_4$ tsp/4 ml Watkins Garlic Powder
$^3/_4$ tsp/4 ml Watkins Lemon Pepper
1 small Watkins Bay Leaf
2 cups/500 ml milk
$^2/_3$ cup/160 ml all-purpose flour
12 ounces/340 g white fish fillets,
   cut into cubes
1 package (6 oz/170 g) tiny frozen cooked
   shrimp, rinsed until thawed
1 can (8 oz/227 g) minced clams in
   clam juice
Watkins Parsley or Dill Weed, for garnish

In medium saucepan, sauté onion and celery in Liquid Spice. Slowly add clam juice and next five ingredients. Bring to a boil; cover and reduce heat. Cook for 15 minutes. Combine milk and flour; mix well. Slowly stir into potato mixture and cook until thickened. Add fish, shrimp, clams and their juice. Simmer but do not boil for an additional 8 to 10 minutes or until fish begins to flake. Serve hot with a sprinkling of parsley or dill weed.

Makes 10 servings.

NUTRITIONAL INFORMATION PER SERVING: Calories 190, Protein 19 g, Carbohydrates 16 g, Fat 6 g, Sat Fat 1 g, Cholesterol 76 mg, Sodium 470 mg, Dietary Fiber 1 g.

QUICK AND EASY SHRIMP
CREOLE SOUP

· · · · · ·

This soup is not only a snap to make, but is also low in fat and calories.

2 cups/500 ml chopped, seeded tomato
1/2 cup/125 ml chopped green bell pepper
1/2 cup/125 ml sliced celery
1 cup/250 ml water
1 can (8 oz/227 g) tomato sauce
2 tbsp/30 ml Watkins Chicken Soup Base
1/2 cup/125 ml uncooked instant rice
2 tsp/10 ml Watkins Onion Flakes
1 tsp/5 ml Watkins Calypso Hot Pepper Sauce
1/4 to 1/2 tsp/1.2 to 2.5 ml Watkins Cajun Pepper, to taste
1 1/2 cups/375 ml (6 oz/170 g) frozen, cooked,
  medium shrimp

Combine all ingredients except shrimp in a medium saucepan. Bring to a boil over medium-high heat. Reduce heat; cover and simmer 10 minutes. Add shrimp. Cover saucepan; cook an additional 3 minutes or until shrimp are thoroughly heated through. Serve with additional hot pepper sauce, if desired.

Makes 6 servings.

NUTRITIONAL INFORMATION PER SERVING: Calories 100, Protein 8 g, Carbohydrates 14 g, Fat 1 g, Sat Fat 0 g, Cholesterol 55 mg, Sodium 610 mg, Dietary Fiber 2 g.

AFRICAN BEEF STEW
· · · · · ·

Although it may sound strange to mix peanut butter and hot pepper, this blend is quite common in West Africa, and is used in Indonesia as well. It makes a deliciously hearty stew, and will fascinate the kids!

2 tsp/10 ml Watkins Onion Liquid Spice
1 pound/454 g beef sirloin, cut into
  1-inch/2.5-cm chunks
1¹/₂ cups/375 ml coarsely chopped onion
2 cups/500 ml water
1 tbsp/15 ml Watkins Chicken Soup Base
¹/₄ cup/60 ml tomato paste
³/₄ tsp/4 ml Watkins Cajun Pepper
¹/₂ cup/125 ml chunky peanut butter
2¹/₂ cups/625 ml cubed butternut squash
  (fresh or frozen)
6 cups/1.5 liters hot cooked rice

In large kettle or Dutch oven, cook beef and onion in Liquid Spice until browned. Add water and next three ingredients. Bring to a boil and simmer 1 hour. Add peanut butter and squash and simmer 10 to 15 minutes or until squash is tender. Serve over hot cooked rice.

Makes 6 servings.

NUTRITIONAL INFORMATION PER SERVING: Calories 620, Protein 34 g, Carbohydrates 77 g, Fat 20 g, Sat Fat 5 g, Cholesterol 58 mg, Sodium 402 mg, Dietary Fiber 6 g.

HERBED POTATO AND LEEK SOUP

· · · · · ·

This peppery potato soup is a great way to start off a holiday feast.

2 tsp/10 ml olive oil
1 tsp/5 ml butter
2¹/₂ cups/625 ml thinly sliced leeks, white part only
*   (about 4 medium)*
2 large shallots, minced
4 cups/1 liter cubed, peeled potatoes
9 cups/2.25 liters water
¹/₃ cup/80 ml Watkins Chicken Soup Base
¹/₂ tsp/2.5 ml Watkins Black Pepper
1 tsp/5 ml Watkins Parsley
³/₄ tsp/4 ml Watkins Basil
Generous pinch Watkins Tarragon

In large saucepan or stockpot, heat oil and butter over low heat. Add leeks and shallots; sauté gently until softened but not brown, 15 to 20 minutes. Add potatoes, water, and next five ingredients. Bring to a boil; reduce heat and simmer, uncovered, until potatoes are tender 15 to 20 minutes. Adjust seasonings to taste.

Makes 12 servings.

NUTRITIONAL INFORMATION PER SERVING: Calories 110, Protein 3 g, Carbohydrates 21 g, Fat 2 g, Sat Fat 0 g, Cholesterol 1 mg, Sodium 380 mg, Dietary Fiber 2 g.

P E P P E R

HAM AND POTATO SOUP

· · · · · ·

A hearty cream soup full of potatoes and ham.

2 cups/500 ml water
2 tsp/10 ml Watkins Chicken Soup Base
4 cups/1 liter peeled and cubed potatoes
2 tsp/10 ml Watkins Onion Liquid Spice
³/₄ cup/180 ml chopped onion
¹/₂ cup/125 ml Watkins Cream Soup Base
¹/₂ cup/125 ml all-purpose flour
1 cup/250 ml milk
1¹/₂ cups/375 ml water
¹/₂ to ³/₄ tsp/2.5 to 4 ml Watkins
  Black Pepper
1 cup/250 ml reserved potato liquid
2 tbsp/30 ml chopped celery leaves
2 cups/500 ml cubed, cooked ham
1 cup/250 ml (4 oz/114 g) shredded
  Cheddar cheese
Celery leaves, for garnish

In large saucepan, bring water and chicken soup base to a boil over medium-high heat. Add potatoes and cook until tender, about 15 minutes. Drain potatoes, reserving 1 cup/250 ml liquid (add water to make 1 cup/250 ml if necessary); set aside. In same saucepan, add Liquid Spice and onions; sauté until tender but not brown. Remove from heat and stir in cream soup base, flour, and milk; mix well. Stir in water. Bring to a boil, over medium heat, stirring constantly. Stir in potatoes, pepper, reserved liquid, celery leaves, ham, and cheese. Reduce heat to low, simmer 30 minutes, stirring frequently. Garnish, if desired.

Makes 8 servings.

NUTRITIONAL INFORMATION PER SERVING: Calories 270, Protein 16 g, Carbohydrates 24 g, Fat 13 g, Sat Fat 4 g, Cholesterol 44 mg, Sodium 1100 mg, Dietary Fiber 2 g.

MEXICAN CHICKEN, CORN AND TORTILLA SOUP

· · · · · ·

Tortilla soups are a tradition in Mexico.
This deliciously spicy soup is well worth the effort it takes to make.

Vegetable oil for frying
8 corn tortillas, halved and cut crosswise
  into strips
1/2 cup/125 ml chopped onion
1 1/2 tsp/7.5 ml Watkins Garlic Powder
1 tbsp/15 ml Watkins Chili Powder
2 1/2 tsp/13 ml Watkins Cumin
1/2 tsp/2.5 ml Watkins Mexican Oregano
1 Watkins Bay Leaf
6 cups/1.5 liters water
1/4 cup/60 ml Watkins Chicken Soup Base
1 can (8 oz/227 g) tomato sauce
1/2 tsp/2.5 ml Watkins Cajun Pepper
1 pound/454 g skinless, boneless,
  chicken breasts
1 1/4 cups/325 ml fresh corn kernels or
  frozen, thawed
1/2 cup/125 ml sour cream
1 tbsp/15 ml Watkins Salsa and Sour Cream
  Dip Mix
Watkins Cilantro, for garnish
Chopped red onion, for garnish
1/4 cup/60 ml fresh corn kernels or
  frozen, thawed, for garnish

Pour oil into a medium skillet to a depth of
3/4 inch/2 cm. Heat oil to 350°F./180°C.

Fry tortilla strips in small batches until
crisp and golden, about 1 minute. Drain on
paper toweling.

Transfer 1 tbsp/15 ml of the tortilla frying
oil to a large kettle or Dutch oven. Add the
onion and sauté until tender. Add garlic
and chili powders, cumin, oregano, and bay
leaf. Sauté 1 minute. Add water, chicken
soup base, tomato sauce, and Cajun Pepper;
bring to a boil. Add chicken; cover and
simmer about 30 minutes or until chicken
is done.

Meanwhile, combine the sour cream and dip
mix; let stand until serving time.

Remove chicken from soup with a slotted
spoon and cool slightly. Shred or chop
finely. Add the 1 1/4 cups/325 ml corn to
soup. Simmer until corn is tender, about 5
minutes. Add chicken and heat through.
To serve, ladle soup into bowls. Garnish
with tortilla strips, salsa dip, cilantro, red
onion, and corn.

Makes 6 servings.

NUTRITIONAL INFORMATION PER SERVING: Calories 290, Protein 24 g, Carbohydrates 34 g, Fat 8 g, Sat Fat 3 g, Cholesterol 52 mg, Sodium 940 mg, Dietary Fiber 6 g.

VEGETARIAN GUMBO

· · · · · ·

Gumbo is a classic Southern dish introduced by the slaves of the 18th and 19th centuries. Not only is the name of African origin, but so is the use of okra for thickening and flavor. This is a much quicker and easier recipe than most, but as with all gumbos, the first step is to make a *roux*...

2 tbsp/30 ml Onion Liquid Spice
¹/₄ cup/60 ml all-purpose flour
2¹/₂ cups/625 ml sliced celery
2 cups/500 ml chopped green pepper
2 cups/500 ml chopped onion
4 cups/1 liter water
2¹/₂ tsp/13 ml Watkins Seasoning Salt
1¹/₂ tsp/7.5 ml Watkins Garlic Flakes
³/₄ to 1 tsp/4 to 5 ml Watkins Cajun Pepper,
  more or less as desired
¹/₄ tsp/1.2 ml Watkins Oregano
1 Watkins Bay Leaf
1 can (15 oz/425 g) black beans, rinsed
  and drained
1 can (16 oz/454 g) black-eyed peas, rinsed
  and drained
1 can (11 oz/312 g) whole kernel corn,
  drained
1 package (10 oz/283 g) frozen cut okra,
  thawed
4 cups/1 liter hot cooked rice
Watkins Calypso Hot Pepper Sauce

In a heavy large saucepan or Dutch oven, heat Liquid Spice over medium heat. Add flour and cook 2 to 3 minutes, stirring constantly with a whisk until mixture is smooth and dark golden brown. Stir in celery, green pepper, and onions; reduce heat to low. Cook 10 minutes, stirring frequently until vegetables are tender.

Slowly add water, stirring frequently, to avoid lumps. Increase heat to medium-high and bring to a boil. Stir in seasoning salt and next seven ingredients; reduce heat and simmer, covered, 15 minutes or until heated through. Stir okra into mixture and cook 3 minutes longer.

Ladle gumbo into soup bowls and add a large spoonful of rice. Pass the hot pepper sauce as a condiment.

Makes 8 servings.

NUTRITIONAL INFORMATION PER SERVING: Calories 340, Protein 13 g, Carbohydrates 66 g, Fat 5 g, Sat Fat 1 g, Cholesterol 0 mg, Sodium 800 mg, Dietary Fiber11 g.

P E P P E R

BEEF PEPPER-POT SOUP

· · · · · ·

Also known as "Philadelphia pepper pot," this soup was said to have been created at Valley Forge during the desperate winter of 1777-1778 when Washington's army was down to tripe, peppercorns and various scraps of other food. As the soup became popular during the late 1700s and early 1800s, it was common to see women selling bowls of it from great kettles on streetcorners, and yelling, "Pepper pot, smokin' hot!"

As those of us developing recipes for this book aren't too keen on tripe, we substituted beef, but you will still get the astounding flavor of pepper in this classic soup. It is common in Philadelphia to serve this dish with dumplings.

5 slices of bacon, diced
1 pound/454 g lean beef stew meat
$^1/_2$ cup/125 ml chopped onion
$^1/_2$ cup/125 ml chopped celery
$^1/_2$ cup/125 ml chopped green onion
2 cups/500 ml chopped green pepper
2 quarts/2 liters water
$^1/_3$ cup/80 ml Watkins Beef Soup Base
$1^1/_4$ tsp/6.5 ml Watkins Black Pepper,
  more if desired
$^1/_2$ tsp/2.5 ml Watkins Thyme
$^1/_2$ tsp/2.5 ml Watkins Ground Cloves
$^1/_4$ tsp/1.2 ml Watkins Red Pepper Flakes
1 Watkins Bay Leaf
1 large potato, diced
$^1/_4$ cup/60 ml butter, melted
$^1/_4$ cup/60 ml all-purpose flour

In a large kettle, sauté the bacon until clear. Add the beef, onion, celery, green onion, and green peppers; sauté until tender. Add the remaining ingredients except potato, butter and flour. Bring to a boil, then turn down to a simmer. Cook, covered, until beef is tender, about $1^1/_2$ hours. Add the diced potato and cook, uncovered, for an additional 20 minutes.

Prepare a *roux* in a small saucepan by stirring the flour into the melted butter and cooking for 1 minute on top of stove. When soup is done, stir in the *roux* and simmer, stirring constantly, until soup begins to thicken. Adjust seasonings to taste.

Makes 8 servings.

NUTRITIONAL INFORMATION PER SERVING: Calories 250, Protein 20 g, Carbohydrates 15 g, Fat 13 g, Sat Fat 6 g, Cholesterol 65 mg, Sodium 890 mg, Dietary Fiber 2 g.

CREAMY ONION SOUP

. . . . . .

Top this rich-tasting soup with crumbled fried bacon and minced green onion.

$^1/_4$ cup/60 ml butter or margarine
6 cups/1.5 liters peeled, quartered and sliced onions
$^3/_4$ cup/180 ml coarsely shredded carrots
1 cup/250 ml Watkins Cream Soup Base
$^1/_2$ cup/125 ml all-purpose flour
3 cups/750 ml water
2 cups/500 ml milk
$^1/_2$ tsp/2.5 ml Watkins Black Pepper
$^1/_2$ tsp/2.5 ml Watkins Garlic Powder
$^1/_4$ tsp/1.2 ml Watkins Thyme
$^1/_8$ tsp/0.6 ml Watkins Nutmeg
Crisp-fried bacon and Watkins Minced Green Onion,
   as toppings

In large saucepan or Dutch oven, sauté onions in butter until crisp-tender and golden brown. Add carrots, cream soup base, flour, and water; mix well. Add remaining ingredients, except toppings, and bring to a boil over medium-high heat, stirring occasionally. Reduce heat and continue to cook until soup begins to thicken. Ladle into serving bowls.

Makes 8 servings.

NUTRITIONAL INFORMATION PER SERVING: Calories 230, Protein 5 g, Carbohydrates 21 g, Fat 16 g, Sat Fat 5 g, Cholesterol 36 mg, Sodium 1010 mg, Dietary Fiber 2 g.

PEPPER

BEEF AND RICE STEW
● ● ● ● ● ●

A hearty stew delicately flavored with rosemary and pepper.

2 pounds/908 g lean beef stew meat
2¼ cups/560 ml water
¼ cup/60 ml red wine vinegar
⅓ cup/80 ml Watkins Beef Soup Base
1 tbsp/15 ml Watkins Parsley
1½ tsp/7.5 ml Watkins Basil
1 tsp/5 ml Watkins Garlic Powder
1 tsp/5 ml Watkins Black Pepper
¾ tsp/4 ml Watkins Rosemary
4 carrots, cut into 1-inch/2.5-cm chunks
12 ounces/340 g fresh mushrooms, cleaned and cut in half,
    if large
1 large onion, coarsely chopped
1 package (8 oz/227 g) brown and wild rice medley
1½ cups/375 ml water
1½ cups/375 ml frozen peas

In large oven-proof kettle or Dutch oven, combine first nine
ingredients. Cover and bake at 375°F./190°C. for 1 hour. Add
carrots, mushrooms, onion, rice medley, and water. Bake an
additional 1 to 1½ hours or until rice and carrots are tender
and stew begins to thicken; remove from oven. Stir in peas;
let stand until peas are heated through.

Makes 8 servings.

NUTRITIONAL INFORMATION PER SERVING: Calories 390, Protein 39 g, Carbohydrates 35 g, Fat 10 g, Sat Fat 3 g,
Cholesterol 94 mg, Sodium 830 mg, Dietary Fiber 6 g.

PEPPERED SALMON STEAKS
· · · · · ·

A lively blend of pepper and ginger highlights this tasty dish.

1 tbsp/15 ml Watkins Cracked Black Pepper
1¹/₄ tsp/6 ml Watkins Ginger
1 tsp/5 ml Watkins Seasoning Salt
4 salmon steaks, cut ³/₄-inch/2-cm thick (about 2 pounds/908 g)
¹/₄ cup/60 ml butter, melted
Lemon slices and parsley, for garnish

Preheat oven to 425°F./220°C. In a small bowl, combine
pepper, ginger, and seasoning salt. Press lightly into both
sides of salmon steaks. Arrange salmon steaks in a single
layer in a greased shallow baking pan. Drizzle with butter.
Bake, basting once with pan juices, until fish is opaque, about
15 minutes. Garnish with lemon slices and parsley. Drizzle
with pan juices.

Makes 4 servings.

NUTRITIONAL INFORMATION PER SERVING: Calories 430, Protein 45 g, Carbohydrates 1 g, Fat 26 g, Sat Fat 9 g,
Cholesterol 156 mg, Sodium 460 mg, Dietary Fiber 0 g.

LEMON PEPPER SCALLOPS

· · · · · ·

Who says gourmet cooking has to be difficult? This easy-to-make dish tastes fabulous! Perfect for a dinner party where you want to impress guests... and spend time with them!

1 pound/454 g large sea scallops
2 tbsp/30 ml butter, melted
2 tbsp/30 ml dried bread crumbs
1 tsp/5 ml Watkins Basil
1 tsp/5 ml Watkins Lemon Pepper
Lemon slices or wedges, for garnish
Fresh parsley or basil, for garnish

Preheat broiler. Rinse scallops with cold water to remove any sand from crevices. Pat dry with paper towels. In medium bowl, toss scallops with melted butter to coat well.

On waxed paper, mix bread crumbs, basil, and lemon pepper. Dip one flat side of each scallop into bread-crumb mixture. Place scallops, breaded-side up, on rack of broiling pan.

With broiler pan at closest position to source of heat, broil scallops 5 minutes, without turning, until crumb topping is golden and scallops are opaque throughout. Arrange on platter. Serve with slices of lemon; garnish with parsley or basil.

Makes 4 servings.

NUTRITIONAL INFORMATION PER SERVING: Calories 170, Protein 20 g, Carbohydrates 6 g, Fat 7 g, Sat Fat 4 g, Cholesterol 53 mg, Sodium 260 mg, Dietary Fiber 0 g.

P E P P E R

FLORIDA FISH FILLETS
· · · · · ·

This colorful, healthful and delicious dish is easily made in the microwave.

1 pound/454 g fish fillets (¹/₄ to ¹/₂-inch/.5 to 1 cm thick),
  thawed if frozen
2 tbsp/30 ml fresh lemon juice
1 cup/250 ml diced tomato, peeled if desired
1 cup/250 ml shredded, unpeeled, zucchini squash
³/₄ to 1 tsp/4 to 5 ml Watkins Lemon Pepper
³/₄ tsp/4 ml Watkins Seasoning Salt
¹/₂ tsp/2.5 ml Watkins Basil, crushed
¹/₄ tsp/1.2 ml Watkins Tarragon, crushed
Lemon twists, for garnish

If necessary, cut fillets in four serving-size pieces. Place in lightly greased 8-inch/20-cm square glass baking dish, with thicker portions toward outside. Turn under any thin portions to obtain an even thickness. Sprinkle with lemon juice; cover with plastic wrap and microwave (HIGH) 4 minutes.

Meanwhile, combine all of the remaining ingredients except lemon twists. Remove fish from microwave and pour off excess juices. Spoon tomato mixture over fish. Recover with plastic wrap and microwave (HIGH) 3 to 4 minutes or until fish flakes easily with fork. Let stand, covered, 4 minutes. Remove fish and vegetables to serving platter with slotted spatula. Garnish with lemon twists.

Makes 4 servings.

NUTRITIONAL INFORMATION PER SERVING: Calories 110, Protein 21 g, Carbohydrates 5 g, Fat 1 g, Sat Fat 0 g, Cholesterol 49 mg, Sodium 270 mg, Dietary Fiber 1 g.

HALIBUT WITH GARDEN-STYLE MARINARA SAUCE

· · · · · ·

A robust tomato sauce accompanies the mild-tasting halibut. Both fish and sauce are easily made in the microwave.

4 fresh or frozen halibut, cod, or shark
   steaks, cut 1 inch/2.5 cm thick (about
   2 pounds/908 g), thawed if frozen
³/₄ tsp/180 ml Watkins Italian Pepper,
   divided
2 small zucchini and/or yellow summer
   squash
1 small onion, halved then thinly sliced
2 tbsp/30 ml water
2 tsp/10 ml Watkins Garlic Powder
1¹/₂ tsp/7.5 ml Watkins Oregano, crushed
1 can (14¹/₂ oz/411 g) diced peeled
   tomatoes
4 tsp/20 ml cornstarch
¹/₈ tsp/0.6 ml Watkins Red Pepper Flakes,
   more if desired
Salt, to taste

Place steaks in an 11-x7-inch/28-x18-cm glass baking dish. Cover with plastic wrap, venting at one corner. Microwave (HIGH) for 6 to 8 minutes or until fish flakes easily, turning and sprinkling with ¹/₄ tsp/1.2 ml Italian Pepper after 3 minutes. Let stand, covered, while preparing sauce.

For sauce, cut zucchini in half lengthwise, then into thin slices. Place in a 2-quart/2-liter casserole along with onion, water, garlic powder, oregano, and remaining ¹/₂ tsp/2.5 ml Italian Pepper. Microwave (HIGH), covered, for 3 minutes or until nearly tender. Stir together tomatoes, cornstarch and red pepper flakes; add to vegetable mixture. Microwave (HIGH) 3 to 4 minutes more or until thickened, stirring every 30 seconds. Add salt, to taste.

To serve, place fish on individual serving plates and spoon sauce over top. If desired, serve with hot cooked couscous or rice.

Makes 4 servings.

NUTRITIONAL INFORMATION PER SERVING: Calories 310, Protein 50 g, Carbohydrates 14 g, Fat 6 g, Sat Fat 1 g, Cholesterol 73 mg, Sodium 290 mg, Dietary Fiber 3 g.

ITALIAN FISH FILLETS

· · · · · ·

Health experts say we all need to eat more fish. That's an easy task to accomplish when the results are this delicious.

1¹/₂ pounds/680 g fresh or frozen fish fillets (such as cod, orange roughy, or haddock), ¹/₂ to ³/₄ inch/2 to 3 cm thick
1 tsp/5 ml Watkins Italian Pepper, divided
³/₄ tsp/4 ml Watkins Garlic Salt, divided
2 cups/500 ml fresh sliced mushrooms (8 oz/227 g)
1 cup/250 ml chopped green pepper
³/₄ cup/180 ml chopped onion
¹/₄ cup/60 ml water
1 can (8 oz/227 g) tomato sauce
1¹/₂ tsp/7.5 ml Watkins Italian Seasoning
4 cups/1 liter hot cooked spinach egg noodles or fettuccine

Thaw fish if frozen. Cut into six serving-sized pieces. Spray a 2-quart/2-liter rectangular baking dish with vegetable cooking spray. Place fish in prepared dish, tucking under any thin edges.

Sprinkle with ¹/₂ tsp/2.5 ml Italian Pepper, and ¹/₄ tsp/1.2 ml garlic salt. Bake fish, uncovered, in a 450°F./235°C. oven just until fish flakes easily with a fork (allow 6 to 9 minutes per ¹/₂ inch/1 cm thickness). Drain off any liquid; keep warm.

Meanwhile, in medium covered saucepan, cook mushrooms, green pepper, and onion in the 1/4 cup/60 ml water about 5 minutes. Drain, add tomato sauce, Italian seasoning, remaining ¹/₂ tsp/2.5 ml each Italian Pepper and garlic salt. Heat through. To serve, divide hot cooked noodles on individual plates. Place fish fillets on top. Evenly spoon sauce over fish.

Makes 6 servings.

NUTRITIONAL INFORMATION PER SERVING: Calories 170, Protein 7 g, Carbohydrates 34 g, Fat 1 g, Sat Fat 0 g, Cholesterol 3 mg, Sodium 410 mg, Dietary Fiber 3 g.

P E P P E R

POISSON AU POIVRE (PEPPERED FISH)
. . . . .

The "surf" version of the "turf" favorite, pepper steak. This is a colorful dish with a peppery bite.

1 pound/454 g fresh or frozen, thawed white fish fillets
  (such as orange roughy, sole, or flounder)
1 tbsp/15 ml butter, melted
1 cup/250 ml coarsely shredded carrot
1 cup/250 ml diced fresh mushrooms
1 1/2 tsp/7.5 ml finely cracked Watkins Garlic Peppercorn Blend
1 tsp/5 ml Watkins Onion Powder
1/4 tsp/1.2 ml salt
Lemon wedges
Fresh parsley or dill

Place fish fillets on a large piece of aluminum foil. Brush top side with melted butter. Spoon carrots, then mushrooms, evenly over fish fillets. Sprinkle with Garlic Peppercorn Blend, onion powder, and salt. Bring edges of foil together and wrap tightly. Place on baking sheet and bake at 350°F./180°C. for 20 to 25 minutes or until fish flakes easily with fork. Carefully remove fillets from foil and place on serving plate. Garnish with lemon wedges and parsley.

Makes 4 servings.

NUTRITIONAL INFORMATION PER SERVING: Calories 150, Protein 22 g, Carbohydrates 4 g, Fat 4 g, Sat Fat 2 g, Cholesterol 62 mg, Sodium 260 mg, Dietary Fiber 1 g.

CITRUS FISH FILLETS WITH LENTILS

· · · · · ·

A delicate citrus flavor enhances both the fish and lentils in this healthful
Mediterranean-style dish.

1 tbsp/15 ml fresh lemon juice
1 tbsp/15 ml fresh orange juice
4 tsp/20 ml olive oil
1/2 tsp/2.5 ml Watkins Lemon Pepper
1 cup/250 ml dried lentils
2 cups/500 ml water
2 1/2 tbsp/40 ml Watkins Chicken Soup Base
1/3 cup/80 ml minced shallots
1/8 tsp/0.6 ml Watkins Lemon Pepper
1 pound/454 g firm white fish fillets, cut into
   4 serving-sized pieces

In small bowl, combine first four ingredients; set aside.

In medium saucepan, combine lentils, water, and chicken
soup base. Bring mixture to a boil; reduce heat and simmer
20 to 25 minutes or until lentils are done but still firm.

Meanwhile, place fish fillets on foil-lined broiler pan.
Drizzle 1 tsp/5 ml of the juice mixture over each fillet. Broil
6 to 8 minutes or until opaque. When lentils are done, add
shallots and lemon pepper; spoon onto serving plate(s) and
top with fish fillets. Drizzle remaining juice mixture over
all. Garnish with fresh parsley, lemon and orange peel strips.

Makes 4 servings.

NUTRITIONAL INFORMATION PER SERVING: Calories 330, Protein 35 g, Carbohydrates 33 g, Fat 7 g, Sat Fat 1 g,
Cholesterol 49 mg, Sodium 600 mg, Dietary Fiber 6 g.

P E P P E R

SPICY LEMON-BAKED SHRIMP
· · · · · ·

Cajun Pepper adds the pizzazz to this recipe. For tamer palates,
just adjust the quantity added.

1/4 cup/60 ml olive oil
3 tbsp/45 ml lemon juice
2 tsp/10 ml honey
2 tsp/10 ml soy sauce
1 1/4 tsp/6 ml Watkins Parsley
1 1/4 tsp/6 ml Watkins Cajun Pepper, less if desired
3/4 tsp/4 ml Watkins Garlic Powder
1 pound/454 g uncooked large shrimp, peeled and deveined
Lemon wedges
French bread

Combine first seven ingredients in 13-x9-inch/33-x23-cm
glass baking dish. Add shrimp; toss to coat. Refrigerate one
hour. Bake at 450°F./235°C. until shrimp are cooked through,
about 6 to 8 minutes, stirring occasionally. Serve shrimp
with lemon wedges and French bread to dip in the zesty
sauce.

Makes 6 servings.

NUTRITIONAL INFORMATION PER SERVING: Calories 170, Protein 16 g, Carbohydrates 3 g, Fat 10 g, Sat Fat 1 g,
Cholesterol 147 mg, Sodium 304 mg, Dietary Fiber 0 g.

SPANISH-STYLE FISH
GRILLED IN FOIL

· · · · · ·

A beautiful and spicy dish that is a snap to make (clean-up is easy, too)!

1½ pounds/681 g cod, halibut or red snapper,
  ½ to 3/4 inch/1 to 1.5 cm thick
¼ cup/60 ml sliced pimento-stuffed olives
2 tsp/10 ml capers
3 green onions, thinly sliced
1 medium tomato, seeded and coarsely chopped
¾ tsp/4 ml Watkins Garlic Salt
2 tbsp/30 ml lemon juice
½ tsp/2.5 ml Watkins Lemon Pepper
½ tsp/2.5 ml Watkins Cumin
⅛ tsp/0.6 ml Watkins Cilantro
Lemon wedges

Place fish on six 12-inch/30-cm squares of foil. Combine
olives and remaining ingredients, except lemon wedges, and
spoon over fish. Bring up ends of foil and wrap securely.
Grill foil packets 15 to 20 minutes or until fish flakes easily
with fork. Serve with lemon wedges.

Makes 6 servings.

NUTRITIONAL INFORMATION PER SERVING: Calories 140, Protein 24 g, Carbohydrates 2 g, Fat 4 g, Sat Fat 0 g,
Cholesterol 36 mg, Sodium 400 mg, Dietary Fiber 1 g.

LEMON AND SAGE COD FILLETS
. . . . .

The pungent, balsamic taste of sage and the tart taste of lemon combine with pepper for a sensational, easy-to-make dish.

4 cod fillets, about $^3/_4$ inch/2 cm thick
  (6 oz/170 g each), thawed if frozen
2 tsp/10 ml Watkins Chicken Soup Base
$^1/_2$ tsp/2.5 ml Watkins Lemon Pepper
1 tbsp/15 ml Watkins Onion Flakes
1 tbsp/15 ml water
1 tsp/5 ml Watkins Sage, divided
8 very thin lemon slices, seeded and
  cut in half
3 tbsp/45 ml butter
$^1/_2$ cup/125 ml water
1 tbsp/15 ml cornstarch
1 tbsp/15 ml water
Lemon wedges

Lightly grease a shallow baking dish large enough to hold fish in a single layer. Season fish with soup base and lemon pepper. Place in prepared dish.

In small bowl, combine onion flakes and the tablespoon of water; let stand 2 to 3 minutes to reconstitute. Sprinkle over fish fillets. Sprinkle with $^1/_2$ tsp/2.5 ml sage. Layer lemon slices on top of fish and sprinkle with remaining sage; dot with butter. Pour water into dish. Bake at 350°F./180°C. for 10 to 12 minutes, basting occasionally with pan juices, just until fish is opaque at its thickest part.

Remove from oven and transfer fish to serving platter. Strain fish juices into a small saucepan and bring to a boil over medium heat. Combine cornstarch and 1 tbsp/15 ml water. Stir into boiling juice until thickened. Serve sauce and lemon wedges with fish.

Makes 4 servings.

NUTRITIONAL INFORMATION PER SERVING: Calories 230, Protein 31 g, Carbohydrates 4 g, Fat 10 g, Sat Fat 6 g, Cholesterol 96 mg, Sodium 310 mg, Dietary Fiber 0 g.

BRAISED MOROCCAN-STYLE CHICKEN
· · · · · ·

A staple of North African cuisine, couscous (KOOS-koos) is granular semolina (coarsely ground durum wheat). Packaged precooked couscous is available in Middle-Eastern markets and larger supermarkets. Watkins Apple Bake Seasoning simplifies the usually staggering array of spices used in Moroccan cooking.

One 3½ to 4-pound/1.5 to 2 kg roasting
  chicken, cut into pieces, skin removed
2 tsp/10 ml Watkins Garlic Salt, divided
2 tbsp/30 ml olive oil
1 large yellow onion, cut into large pieces
2½ tsp/12.5 ml Watkins Apple Bake
  Seasoning
½ tsp/2.5 ml Watkins Black Pepper
3 cups/750 ml water
1 cup/250 ml baby peeled carrots
1 medium sweet red or green pepper,
  cut into 1-inch/2.5-cm squares
3 small zucchini, sliced ½-inch/1-cm thick
1 can (15 oz/425 g) garbanzo beans, drained
  and rinsed
1¼ cups/325 ml couscous
Watkins Cilantro and Calypso Hot
  Pepper Sauce

Sprinkle chicken with 1 tsp/5 ml of the garlic salt, set aside. Heat oil in large kettle or Dutch oven. Add onion and sauté until soft. Stir in Apple Bake Seasoning and pepper; sauté 2 minutes longer. Add the chicken and turn until lightly coated with the spices. Add the water and remaining garlic salt; bring to a boil. Reduce the heat to low, cover, and simmer for 30 minutes. Stir in the carrots and simmer 10 minutes. Stir in the red pepper and zucchini. Cover and simmer an additional 5 minutes. Add the garbanzo beans and simmer, uncovered, 2 to 3 minutes or until heated through. With a slotted spoon, transfer the chicken and vegetables to a platter; keep warm. Add the couscous to the Dutch oven, remove from heat. Cover and let stand 5 minutes or until tender. Spoon couscous onto serving plate and place chicken and vegetables on top. Sprinkle with cilantro and pass with hot pepper sauce.

Makes 6 servings.

NUTRITIONAL INFORMATION PER SERVING: Calories 580, Protein 74 g, Carbohydrates 40 g, Fat 8 g, Sat Fat 3 g, Cholesterol 212 mg, Sodium 717 mg, Dietary Fiber 8 g.

MEXICAN CHICKEN AND RICE
• • • • • •

A hearty chicken and rice dish with a Southwestern flair.

1¹/₂ tsp/7.5 ml Watkins Garlic Liquid Spice
1 cup/250 ml chopped onion
¹/₂ cup/125 ml chopped green pepper
1 can (15.5 oz/439 g) kidney, pinto, or
    black beans, drained and rinsed
1 can (14.5 oz/411 g) diced tomatoes
    with juice
1 can (4.5 oz/127 g) diced green chiles
1³/₄ cups/440 ml water
1 tbsp/15 ml Watkins Chicken Soup Base
1 tbsp/15 ml Watkins Mexican Blend
    Seasoning
¹/₄ to ¹/₂ tsp/1.2 to 2.5 ml Watkins
    Black Pepper
³/₄ cup/180 ml uncooked long grain rice
2 cups/500 ml frozen corn
3 tbsp/45 ml all-purpose flour
1 tbsp/15 ml Watkins Paprika
1 tsp/5 ml Watkins Garlic Salt
¹/₄ to ¹/₂ tsp/1.2 to 2.5 ml Watkins
    Black Pepper
2 pounds/908 g skinless, boneless chicken
    breast halves

In large nonstick skillet, sauté onion and green pepper in Liquid Spice until crisp-tender. Place in a large bowl along with beans and next eight ingredients; mix well and place in glass 13-x9-inch/33-x23-cm baking dish.

Combine flour and next three ingredients in a large plastic bag. Add chicken breasts and shake until evenly coated. Place chicken on top of the rice mixture. Cover with foil and bake at 375°F./190°C. for 1 hour and 15 minutes. Remove foil and bake 15 minutes longer or until chicken is lightly browned and the liquid is absorbed into rice. Serve hot.

Makes 8 servings.

NUTRITIONAL INFORMATION PER SERVING: Calories 320, Protein 34 g, Carbohydrates 39 g, Fat 3 g, Sat Fat 0 g, Cholesterol 65 mg, Sodium 810 mg, Dietary Fiber 9 g.

CALIFORNIA CHICKEN KEBABS
. . . . .

With its sunny climate and vast citrus groves, California has long been the epicenter of Mediterranean-style cooking in North America. These chunks of chicken are marinated Greek-style in a tangy lemon and honey mixture, then threaded on skewers with slices of onion and green and red peppers.

¹/₄ cup/60 ml lemon juice
3 tbsp/45 ml honey
2 tbsp/30 ml vegetable oil
1¹/₂ tsp/7.5 ml coarsely cracked Watkins
*   Garlic Peppercorn Blend*
1 tsp/5 ml Watkins Oregano
1 tsp/5 ml Watkins Seasoning Salt,
*   or to taste*
2 pounds/908 g skinless, boneless chicken
*   breasts, cut into 1¹/₂-inch/4-cm pieces*
2 medium-sized red onions
2 green bell peppers
2 red or yellow bell peppers

Prepare marinade by combining first six ingredients in a large bowl. Add the chicken cubes and toss to coat. Let chicken marinate while preparing the vegetables.

Cut onions into large chunks and separate into layers. Halve, seed, and cut the peppers into 1 to 2-inch/1 to 2.5-cm squares.

Remove chicken from marinade; reserving the marinade. Alternately thread pieces of chicken, green and red peppers, and the onion onto 16 skewers. Brush the skewered chicken and vegetables with some of the reserved marinade. Grill or broil the kebabs for 5 minutes. Turn, brush with marinade, and grill or broil for an additional 5 to 6 minutes or until the chicken is cooked and vegetables are crisp-tender.

Makes 8 servings.

NUTRITIONAL INFORMATION PER SERVING: Calories 210, Protein 27 g, Carbohydrates 13 g, Fat 5 g, Sat Fat 1 g, Cholesterol 65 mg, Sodium 210 mg, Dietary Fiber 1 g.

CAJUN CHICKEN PITAS
· · · · · ·

The bayou meets the Eastern Mediterranean in this spicy quick-to-make sandwich.
Add a comforting touch of home by serving it with a bowl of
Watkins Chicken Noodle Soup.

2 tsp/10 ml Watkins Cajun Pepper,
　less if desired
$^1/_2$ tsp/2.5 ml salt, if desired
4 skinless, boneless chicken breast halves
　(about 4 oz/113 g each), cut into
　$^1/_2$-inch/1-cm strips
2 tsp/10 ml Watkins Onion Liquid Spice,
　divided
1 medium onion, halved and thinly sliced
2 whole wheat pita bread rounds, cut in half
2 cups/500 ml loosely-packed shredded
　leaf lettuce
1 cup/250 ml coarsely-chopped tomato
Watkins Inferno or Calypso Hot Pepper
　Sauce, if desired

Combine Cajun Pepper and salt; toss with chicken strips. Heat 1 tsp/5 ml of the Liquid Spice in large nonstick skillet until hot. Add chicken; cook 2 to 3 minutes until chicken is golden brown and done, stirring occasionally. Remove chicken and keep warm. Add remaining Liquid Spice to skillet. Add onion and sauté 1 minute. Reduce heat to medium and cook 5 minutes more or until tender, stirring occasionally. Return chicken to skillet and toss along with onions. Line each pita half with $^1/_2$ cup/125 ml shredded lettuce. Evenly divide chicken mixture and tomatoes between each. Serve with hot pepper sauce.

Makes 4 servings.

NUTRITIONAL INFORMATION PER SERVING: Calories 210, Protein 29 g, Carbohydrates 14 g, Fat 4 g, Sat Fat 1 g, Cholesterol 65 mg, Sodium 470 mg, Dietary Fiber 1 g.

MUSTARD CURRIED CHICKEN
· · · · · ·

Mustard seeds are a common ingredient in Indian curries. Watkins Country Mill Mustard helps create this sweet and spicy curried chicken. Garnish with chopped green onion or fresh parsley or cilantro.

$^1/_4$ cup/60 ml Watkins Country Mill Coarse Ground Mustard
$^1/_4$ cup/60 ml apple juice
2 tbsp/30 ml butter, melted
2 to 3 tsp/10 to 15 ml Watkins Curry Powder, to taste
$^1/_2$ to $^3/_4$ tsp/2.5 to 4 ml Watkins Cajun Pepper, to taste
$1^1/_2$ tsp/7.5 ml Watkins Garlic Salt
6 skinless, boneless chicken breast halves
   (about $1^1/_2$ pounds/680 g)
3 cups hot cooked rice (preferably basmati)

In a shallow baking dish, combine first six ingredients; mix well. Add chicken breast halves, turning to coat. Arrange in a single layer. Bake, uncovered, at 350°F./180°C. for 25 to 30 minutes or until chicken is tender and no longer pink. Place hot cooked rice on serving platter. Top with chicken breasts, spooning pan drippings over all.

Makes 6 servings.

NUTRITIONAL INFORMATION PER SERVING: Calories 330, Protein 30 g, Carbohydrates 35 g, Fat 6 g, Sat Fat 3 g, Cholesterol 76 mg, Sodium 690 mg, Dietary Fiber 3 g.

GRILLED CHICKEN KEBABS
WITH CHICK-PEA SKORDALIA
· · · · · ·

Skordalia is a thick Greek sauce or dip usually made of mashed potatoes, olive oil, and garlic. This version, with chick-peas, is much like the Lebanese dip *hummus*, and makes for an interesting Eastern Mediterranean hybrid dish.

KEBABS
· · · · · ·

3/4 cup/180 ml plain yogurt
1/4 cup/60 ml lemon juice
2 tsp/10 ml Watkins Cracked Black Pepper
1 tsp/5 ml Watkins Garlic Powder
1 tsp/5 ml Watkins Rosemary,
  lightly crushed
1 tsp/5 ml Watkins Cumin
2 pounds/908 g skinless boneless chicken
  breasts, cut into 1-inch/2.5-cm cubes

SKORDALIA
· · · · · ·

1 can (15 1/2 oz/439 g) chick-peas
  (garbanzos) drained, reserving
  1/4 cup/60 ml of the liquid
2 tbsp/30 ml extra-virgin olive oil
2 tbsp/30 ml lemon juice
3/4 tsp/4 ml Watkins Garlic Liquid Spice
1/4 tsp/1.2 ml Watkins Black Pepper,
  or to taste
1/8 tsp/0.6 ml salt, or to taste
2 tsp/10 ml Watkins Parsley

---

1 red onion, cut into wedges, separated
  into "petals"
12 cherry tomatoes
Pita rounds, cut in half

For kebabs, combine the first six ingredients; pour over chicken cubes in shallow glass dish. Cover and chill at least 3 hours or overnight.

For *skordalia*, in food processor or blender, blend chick-peas with their reserved liquid, olive oil, lemon juice, Liquid Spice, pepper, and salt until smooth. Place in serving bowl. (Can be made up to 4 hours ahead. Cover, let stand at room temperature.)

Prepare barbecue grill or preheat broiler. Thread chicken cubes onto skewers alternately with onions, and cherry tomatoes. Grill or broil until done. Serve with *skordalia* and pita bread.

Makes 6 servings.

NUTRITIONAL INFORMATION PER SERVING: Calories 360, Protein 43 g, Carbohydrates 24 g, Fat 9 g, Sat Fat 2 g, Cholesterol 90 mg, Sodium 170 mg, Dietary Fiber 5 g.

BAKED CAJUN CHICKEN

· · · · · ·

This low-fat chicken recipe can be made as spicy as you like by adjusting the quantity of Cajun Pepper used.

2 pounds/908 g meaty chicken pieces, skin removed
Vegetable cooking spray
2 tbsp/30 ml skim milk
1¹/₂ tsp/7.5 ml Watkins Cajun Pepper
³/₄ tsp/4 ml Watkins Garlic Salt
¹/₂ tsp/2.5 ml Watkins Onion Powder
¹/₂ tsp/2.5 ml Watkins Thyme, crushed

Rinse chicken, pat dry. Spray a 13-x9-inch/33-x23-cm baking dish with cooking spray. Arrange chicken, meaty sides up, in dish. Brush with milk.

In small bowl, combine remaining ingredients; sprinkle over chicken. Bake at 375°F./190°C. for 45 to 55 minutes or until chicken is tender and no longer pink. Garnish, if desired, with sliced red, green, or yellow chile peppers.

Makes 4 servings.

NUTRITIONAL INFORMATION PER SERVING: Calories 270, Protein 50 g, Carbohydrates 1 g, Fat 5 g, Sat Fat 1 g, Cholesterol 150 mg, Sodium 470 mg, Dietary Fiber 0 g.

FRENCH QUARTER CHICKEN JAMBALAYA

. . . . . .

Jambalaya is a classic Cajun dish that combines rice, tomatoes, onion, green peppers, and almost any kind of meat, poultry, or shellfish. Try to find *andouille*, the wonderfully spicy Louisiana sausage.

1 pound/454 g skinned, boned chicken cut into 1-inch/2.5-cm cubes
$1/4$ tsp/1.2 ml Watkins Cajun Pepper
1 tbsp/15 ml vegetable oil
1 pound/454 g andouille, kielbasa or other smoked sausage, cut into $1/2$ inch/1-cm slices
1 cup/250 ml coarsely chopped onion
1 cup/250 ml coarsely chopped celery
1 cup/250 ml coarsely chopped green pepper
1 can (16 oz/454g) whole tomatoes, undrained and chopped
1 tbsp/15 ml Watkins Chicken Soup Base
$1^{1}/_2$ cups/375 ml water
1 can (6 oz/170 g) tomato paste
$3/4$ cup/180 ml uncooked regular white rice
1 tbsp/15 ml Watkins Paprika
1 tsp/5 ml Watkins Chicken Seasoning
1 tsp/5 ml Watkins Thyme
1 tsp/5 ml Watkins Garlic Flakes
$1/4$ to $1/2$ tsp/1.2 to 2.5 ml Watkins Cajun Pepper, to taste
1 Watkins Bay Leaf

Sprinkle chicken with $1/4$ tsp/1.2 ml Cajun Pepper. In large Dutch oven or kettle, brown chicken in oil. Remove with slotted spoon and drain on paper toweling; set aside. Add sausage to same Dutch oven and cook until lightly browned. Remove with slotted spoon and drain on paper toweling; set aside.

Sauté onions, celery, and green pepper in same Dutch oven until tender, scraping off any hardened drippings in pan. Add chicken, sausage, and remaining ingredients to vegetables and bring to a boil. Reduce heat; simmer 40 to 45 minutes or until rice is tender. Remove bay leaf before serving.

Makes 6 servings.

NUTRITIONAL INFORMATION PER SERVING: Calories 490, Protein 32 g, Carbohydrates 35 g, Fat 25 g, Sat Fat 8 g, Cholesterol 93 mg, Sodium 1220 mg, Dietary Fiber 4 g.

KALAMATA OLIVE CHICKEN PARMESAN

· · · · · ·

A wonderful entrée marrying classic Mediterranean ingredients. The deep-purple Greek *kalamata* olives give this dish a robust flavor. Canned ripe olives may be substituted, but are not nearly as satisfying.

$^1/_4$ *cup/60 ml dry bread crumbs*
$^1/_4$ *cup/60 ml grated Parmesan cheese*
$^1/_2$ *tsp/2.5 ml Watkins Basil*
$^1/_4$ *tsp/1.2 ml Watkins Italian Pepper*
4 skinless, boneless chicken breast halves
1 egg, beaten
2 tbsp/30 ml olive oil
1 can (15 oz/425 g) tomato sauce
$1^1/_2$ *tsp/7.5 ml Watkins Italian Seasoning*
$^1/_2$ *tsp/2.5 ml Watkins Italian Pepper*
$^1/_2$ *cup/125 ml water*
$^3/_4$ *cup/180 ml chopped red onion*
$^1/_2$ *cup/125 ml chopped* kalamata *or*
  ripe olives
8 ounces/227 g dry fettucine noodles
1 tbsp/15 ml olive oil
$^1/_4$ *cup/60 ml grated Parmesan cheese*

Combine first four ingredients; mix well. Dip each chicken breast half in egg, then coat with bread crumb mixture. Heat 2 tbsp/30 ml oil in large skillet over medium-high heat. Add chicken and brown well on both sides. Add tomato sauce and next three ingredients. Cover, cook over low heat 15 to 20 minutes or until chicken is no longer pink and juices run clear, stirring occasionally. Add onions and olives; cook an additional 5 minutes.

Meanwhile, cook fettuccine per label directions; drain. Toss with 1 tbsp/15 ml olive oil; place on serving platter and spoon chicken/olive mixture over top. Sprinkle with Parmesan cheese.

Makes 4 servings.

NUTRITIONAL INFORMATION PER SERVING: Calories 590, Protein 42 g, Carbohydrates 60 g, Fat 21 g, Sat Fat 4 g, Cholesterol 130 mg, Sodium 1190 mg, Dietary Fiber 2 g.

CAJUN TURKEY BURGERS
· · · · · ·

The zesty topping gives these burgers an extra flavor boost.

¹/₂ cup/125 ml reduced-calorie mayonnaise
2 tbsp/30 ml Watkins Inferno Hot Pepper Sauce
1 pound/454 g ground raw turkey or chicken
¹/₄ cup/60 ml finely chopped green pepper
2 tbsp/30 ml quick-cooking oatmeal
1 tsp/5 ml Watkins Onion Flakes reconstituted
  with 1 tsp/5 ml water
¹/₂ tsp/2.5 ml Watkins Garlic Salt
¹/₂ tsp/2.5 ml Watkins Cajun Pepper
4 large whole-wheat hamburger buns
Lettuce and tomato, for garnish

Combine mayonnaise and Inferno sauce; set aside. Combine
turkey and next five ingredients; mix well and shape into
four patties, each about ¹/₂ inch/1 cm thick.

Grill or broil patties until done and no longer pink inside,
turning once. Place on buns, topping with lettuce and tomato.
Spread top half of bun with mayonnaise mixture and place
on top of burger.

Makes 4 servings.

NUTRITIONAL INFORMATION PER SERVING: Calories 440, Protein 24 g, Carbohydrates 28 g, Fat 26 g, Sat Fat 7 g,
Cholesterol 93 mg, Sodium 1030 mg, Dietary Fiber 1 g.

ROAST TURKEY BREAST

· · · · · ·

The oven cooking bag helps retain the turkey's juiciness and flavor.

One 5-pound/2.3-kg turkey breast, skin removed
1 medium onion, quartered
2 ribs celery, halved
Vegetable cooking spray
1½ tbsp/25 ml Watkins Lemon Pepper
2 tsp/10 ml Watkins Garlic Powder
2 tsp/10 ml Watkins Onion Powder
1 tsp/5 ml Watkins Poultry Seasoning
1 tsp/5 ml salt, or to taste
½ tsp/2.5 ml Watkins Paprika
Oven cooking bag

Rinse turkey breast; pat dry with paper toweling. Place onion and celery in breast cavity. Spray turkey breast with cooking spray. Combine remaining ingredients and rub into turkey breast. Place in oven cooking bag prepared per package directions; place in shallow baking dish. Bake at 325°F./165°C. for 1 hour. Cut a slit in top of bag. Insert meat thermometer. Bake an additional hour or until thermometer registers 170°F./75°C. Transfer to large platter. If desired, thicken drippings in bag to make a gravy to accompany sliced turkey. Garnish with fresh parsley sprigs.

Makes 10 servings.

NUTRITIONAL INFORMATION PER SERVING: Calories 290, Protein 55 g, Carbohydrates 2 g, Fat 6 g, Sat Fat 2 g, Cholesterol 126 mg, Sodium 350 mg, Dietary Fiber 0 g.

P E P P E R

PASTA WITH LEMON-PEPPERED CHICKEN

· · · · · ·

Use spinach linguine or other vegetable-flavored pasta to add color
to this savory dish.

1 pound/454 g skinless, boneless chicken breasts,
  cut into ½-inch/1-cm strips
2 tsp/30 ml Watkins Cracked Black Pepper
1½ tsp/7.5 ml Watkins Garlic Liquid Spice
2 tbsp/30 ml olive oil
1½ cups/375 ml water
2 tbsp/30 ml Watkins Chicken Soup Base
1½ tbsp/25 ml fresh lemon juice, or to taste
12 oz/340 g dry ribbon noodles, such as linguine
½ cup/125 ml finely grated Parmesan cheese

Toss the chicken with the cracked pepper and Liquid Spice.
Marinate, covered and refrigerated, for at least one hour or
as long as overnight.

When ready to serve, bring water to boil to cook pasta. Heat
olive oil in a sauté pan over medium-high heat. Add chicken
and lightly brown on all sides, about 3 minutes. Add the
water, chicken soup base, and lemon juice. Reduce heat to a
simmer and cook for about 8 minutes.

Cook pasta; drain and toss with chicken. Serve dish hot,
passing Parmesan cheese separately. Garnish with lemon
wedges and fresh parsley.

Makes 6 servings.

NUTRITIONAL INFORMATION PER SERVING: Calories 380, Protein 28 g, Carbohydrates 43 g, Fat 10 g, Sat Fat 2 g,
Cholesterol 49 mg, Sodium 450 mg, Dietary Fiber 0 g.

CAJUN-STYLE BARBECUED RIBS
· · · · · ·

Serve these scrumptious ribs with corn on the cob, coleslaw, and lemonade for a summer meal that can't be beat.

2 tsp/10 ml Watkins Chili Powder
2 tsp/10 ml Watkins Dry Mustard
1 tsp/5 ml Watkins Cajun Pepper
1 tsp/5 ml Watkins Garlic Salt
4 pounds/1.8 kg pork loin back ribs
   or baby-back ribs
Sweet and Spicy Glaze (recipe follows)

Mix first four ingredients together; sprinkle and rub into ribs. Place over indirect heat on grill or in 350°F./180°C. oven. Cook 50 to 60 minutes, brushing pork with glaze the last 15 minutes of grilling, or until pork is no longer pink in center. Heat any remaining glaze to boiling and serve with ribs.

Makes 8 servings.

SWEET AND SPICY GLAZE
· · · · · ·

1/2 cup/125 ml Watkins Inferno Hot
   Pepper Sauce
2 to 3 tbsp/30 to 45 ml brown sugar, to taste
1/2 tsp/2.5 ml Watkins Garlic Liquid Spice
1/4 tsp/1.2 ml Watkins Cajun Pepper

In small saucepan, bring all ingredients just to a boil; remove from heat.

NUTRITIONAL INFORMATION PER SERVING: Calories 440, Protein 20 g, Carbohydrates 10 g, Fat 35 g, Sat Fat 20 g, Cholesterol 210 mg, Sodium 690 mg, Dietary Fiber 0 g.

GARLIC-PEPPER PORK LOIN WITH LEMON-DILL MUSTARD SAUCE
· · · · ·

This tangy mustard sauce is also a wonderful accompaniment to broiled salmon steaks or fillets, fish or chicken.

3 pounds/1.3 kg boneless pork loin roast, rolled and tied
2 tbsp/30 ml vegetable oil
2 tsp/10 ml Watkins Garlic Salt
2 tsp/10 ml coarsely crushed Watkins Garlic Peppercorn Blend (more if desired)
Lemon-Dill Mustard Sauce (recipe follows)

Place roast in large shallow bowl. Rub in oil, garlic salt, and Garlic Peppercorn Blend; coating roast well. Refrigerate at least one hour or overnight. Grill over indirect heat or bake at 325°F./165°C. for 1 to 1 1/2 hours or until meat thermometer registers 160°F./71°C. Remove to serving platter, let stand 10 minutes, then slice and serve with Lemon-Dill Mustard Sauce.

Makes 8 servings.

LEMON-DILL MUSTARD SAUCE
· · · · ·

1 cup/250 ml mayonnaise
1/4 cup/60 ml Parisienne Mustard
1 1/2 to 2 tsp/7.5 to 10 ml Watkins Lemon-Dill Liquid Spice
1 tsp/5 ml Watkins Parsley

In small bowl, combine all ingredients; mix until smooth. Cover and refrigerate up to 24 hours. Let stand at room temperature 30 minutes before serving.

Makes 1 1/4 cups/325 ml.

NUTRITIONAL INFORMATION PER SERVING: Calories 630, Protein 48 g, Carbohydrates 3 g, Fat 45 g, Sat Fat 10 g, Cholesterol 180 mg, Sodium 780 mg, Dietary Fiber 0 g.

PICANTE PORK CHOPS
· · · · · ·

An unique flavor combination for those who enjoy spicy Mexican food.

4 boneless pork chops, each cut ³/₄-inch/
  2 cm thick (about 2 pounds/908 g)
¹/₂ to ³/₄ tsp/2.5 to 3.8 ml Watkins
  Cajun Pepper, to taste
¹/₂ tsp/2.5 ml Watkins Mexican Oregano
1 tbsp/15 ml vegetable oil
1¹/₄ cups/320 ml water
1¹/₂ tbsp/25 ml Watkins Chicken
  Soup Base
3 tbsp/45 ml lime juice
1 tbsp/15 ml sugar
2 tbsp/30 ml Watkins Jalapeño Mustard
1¹/₂ tbsp/2.5 ml cornstarch
2 tbsp/30 ml water
4 cups/1 liter hot cooked rice
Fresh lime slices and parsley, for garnish

Sprinkle chops with a mixture of the Cajun Pepper and Mexican oregano. Place oil in large skillet over medium heat; cook chops until browned on both sides, about 10 minutes. Spoon off fat. Stir in water and next four ingredients; bring to a boil. Reduce heat to low; cover and cook 15 to 20 minutes or until fork-tender, turning occasionally.

Transfer chops to a platter; keep warm. In small bowl, combine cornstarch and water; mix until smooth. Gradually stir into skillet. Cook mixture over high heat until mixture begins to boil and thicken, stirring constantly. To serve, place rice on platter. Top with pork chops, spooning sauce over all. Garnish with lime slices and parsley.

Makes 4 servings.

NUTRITIONAL INFORMATION PER SERVING: Calories 860, Protein 79 g, Carbohydrates 63 g, Fat 28 g, Sat Fat 9 g, Cholesterol 220 mg, Sodium 730 mg, Dietary Fiber 1 g.

PORK TENDERLOIN WITH BRAISED RED CABBAGE

· · · · · ·

Caraway seeds have a nutty, delicate anise-like flavor and are widely used in German, Austrian, and Hungarian dishes.

1¹/₂ pounds/680 g pork tenderloin, trimmed of fat and membrane
¹/₂ tsp/2.5 ml Watkins Sage
¹/₂ tsp/2.5 ml Watkins Seasoning Salt
1 tsp/5 ml Watkins Black Pepper, divided
1¹/₂ tsp/7.5 ml caraway seeds
1 tbsp/15 ml Watkins Onion Liquid Spice, divided
1 red onion, thinly sliced
8 cups/2 liters coarsely shredded red cabbage
1 Granny Smith apple, cored and grated
1 cup/250 ml water
1¹/₂ tbsp/7.5 ml Watkins Chicken Soup Base
3 tbsp/45 ml red wine vinegar
1 tbsp/15 ml white sugar
1 Watkins Bay Leaf

Preheat oven to 425°F/220°C. Combine sage, seasoning salt, and ³/₄ tsp/4 ml pepper; rub over all sides of tenderloin. Sprinkle evenly on all sides with caraway seeds. In a large nonstick skillet, heat 2 tsp/10 ml of the Liquid Spice. Brown pork for about 2 minutes on each side and place in a lightly oiled roasting pan. Roast for 10 to 15 minutes or just until meat thermometer registers 160°F./70°C.

Meanwhile in same skillet, heat remaining 1 tsp/5 ml Liquid Spice over low heat. Sauté onions until soft, about 5 to 7 minutes. Add remaining ingredients along with ¹/₄ tsp/1.2 ml pepper and simmer, uncovered, for 10 to 15 minutes, tossing occasionally, until cabbage is tender and most of the liquid has evaporated. Discard bay leaf and adjust seasonings. Carve the pork into ³/₄-inch/2-cm-thick slices and serve with braised cabbage.

Makes 6 servings.

NUTRITIONAL INFORMATION PER SERVING: Calories 230, Protein 26 g, Carbohydrates 18 g, Fat 6 g, Sat Fat 2 g, Cholesterol 73 mg, Sodium 370 mg, Dietary Fiber 4 g.

PINEAPPLE PORK CHOPS

· · · · · ·

Accompany this sweetly-glazed pork with hot cooked rice.

4 butterflied boneless pork chops (about
  6 oz/170 g each), trimmed of excess fat
1¹/₂ tsp/7.5 ml Watkins Garlic Salt,
  divided
¹/₂ tsp/2.5 ml Watkins Black Pepper,
  more if desired
2 tsp/10 ml Watkins Onion Liquid Spice
1 green bell pepper, cut into strips
¹/₂ cup/125 ml red onion slices
1 can (8 oz/227 g) pineapple chunks in own
  juice; drained, juice reserved
Water
1 tbsp/15 ml cornstarch
1 tbsp/15 ml water

Season pork chops with 1 tsp/5 ml garlic salt and the pepper. Heat Liquid Spice in large nonstick skillet over medium-high heat until hot. Add chops and brown on each side. Remove chops from pan; keep warm. Add bell pepper strips and onion slices to skillet. Cook until crisp-tender, stirring and tossing frequently; remove from pan and keep warm.

In measuring cup, combine reserved pineapple juice and enough water to make 1 cup/250 ml. Add to skillet along with remaining ¹/₂ tsp/2.5 ml of garlic salt. Return chops to skillet and simmer, covered, 10 to 15 minutes or until pork chops are done; remove from skillet and keep warm.

Combine cornstarch and water and pour mixture into skillet; cook until thickened and bubbly. Return vegetables and pineapple chunks to skillet; heat through. Serve sauce over warm chops.

Makes 4 servings.

NUTRITIONAL INFORMATION PER SERVING: Calories 540, Protein 56 g, Carbohydrates 13 g, Fat 27 g, Sat Fat 9 g, Cholesterol 179 mg, Sodium 660 mg, Dietary Fiber 1 g.

PORK AND SAUERKRAUT DINNER

· · · · · ·

Serve this delicious "comfort food" with mounds of hot mashed potatoes. Watkins Düsseldorf Mustard makes a great accompaniment to this dish.

3 pounds/1.4 kg sauerkraut (canned or refrigerated)
One 3 to 3¹/₂-pound/1.4 to 1.6-kg pork loin roast
1 can (14.5 oz/411 g) diced tomatoes
2 carrots, cut into sticks
3 celery ribs, sliced into 1-inch/2.5-cm pieces
1 onion, cut into wedges
1 large red apple, cored and cut into wedges
¹/₂ cup/125 ml brown sugar
2 Watkins Bay Leaves
1 tsp/5 ml Watkins Cracked Black Pepper, more if desired
¹/₂ tsp/2.5 ml Watkins Oregano

Place half of the sauerkraut in the bottom of a roasting pan; add pork loin. Put remaining sauerkraut over pork. Pour tomatoes over pork. Add carrots, celery, onion, and apple around edges of roasting pan. Sprinkle brown sugar and seasonings over all.

Cover and cook in a 325°F./165°C. over for 3 to 3¹/₂ hours or until meat is done, basting frequently with pan juices. Slice and serve hot.

Makes 8 servings.

NUTRITIONAL INFORMATION PER SERVING: Calories 620, Protein 67 g, Carbohydrates 32 g, Fat 25 g, Sat Fat 8 g, Cholesterol 225 mg, Sodium 1440 mg, Dietary Fiber 6 g.

P E P P E R

PEPPER-CRUSTED PORK TENDERLOIN
. . . . . .

Serve this spicy dish with mashed potatoes and steamed broccoli.

2 tsp/10 ml Watkins Black Pepper
1³/₄ tsp/9 ml Watkins Garlic Salt
1¹/₄ tsp/6 ml Watkins Italian Seasoning
1 pound/454 g pork tenderloin,
   trimmed of fat
1 tbsp/15 ml olive oil

1¹/₂ tsp/7.5 ml Watkins Beef Soup Base
¹/₂ tsp/Watkins Paprika
¹/₄ to ¹/₂ tsp/1.2 to 2.5 ml Watkins Cracked
   Black Pepper, to taste
¹/₂ cup/125 ml water
¹/₂ cup/125 ml evaporated milk

Combine first three ingredients and rub into pork; let stand 15 minutes. Preheat oven to 400°F./205°C. Heat oil in heavy ovenproof skillet over high heat. Add the pork and brown on all sides, about 4 minutes. Transfer skillet with pork to oven and roast about 20 minutes or until pork is cooked through (160°F./70°C. on meat thermometer), turning occasionally.

Meanwhile, in heavy saucepan, add remaining ingredients and cook over medium heat until mixture is reduced to ¹/₂ cup/125 ml and begins to thicken slightly. Slice pork tenderloin just prior to serving and serve with sauce.

Makes 4 servings.

NUTRITIONAL INFORMATION PER SERVING: Calories 210, Protein 26 g, Carbohydrates 5 g, Fat 9 g, Sat Fat 2 g, Cholesterol 82 mg, Sodium 840 mg, Dietary Fiber 0 g.

SPICED SAUTÉED PORK
AND VEGETABLES
· · · · · ·

This quick and delicious skillet dinner, with its blend of sweet potatoes, tomatoes, dried apricots, and curry-style spices, is reminiscent of West African cooking. It's also a good source of beta carotene and iron.

2 tbsp/30 ml all-purpose flour
1 tsp/5 ml Watkins Cajun Pepper, divided
1 tsp/5 ml Cumin
1 tsp/5 ml Ginger
1/8 tsp/0.6 ml Watkins Cinnamon
1 pound/454 g pork tenderloin, cut into 1/2-inch/1-cm pieces
3 tbsp/45 ml vegetable oil
2 sweet potatoes or yams (about 12 oz/340g)
1 small onion, thinly sliced
1 can (14.5 oz/411 g) stewed tomatoes
1/2 cup/125 ml dried apricots, julienned

Combine flour, 1/4 tsp/1.2 ml Cajun Pepper, and next three ingredients; mix well. Add pork and toss to coat. In skillet, over high heat, sauté pork slices in hot oil until browned on all sides. Add sweet potatoes and onions, sauté 5 minutes. Add tomatoes, remaining 3/4 tsp/4 ml Cajun Pepper, and apricots; reduce heat to medium. Cover and continue to cook, stirring occasionally, 5 minutes or until sweet potatoes are tender.

Makes 4 servings.

NUTRITIONAL INFORMATION PER SERVING: Calories 400, Protein 27 g, Carbohydrates 44 g, Fat 13 g, Sat Fat 7 g,
Cholesterol 73 mg, Sodium 360 mg, Dietary Fiber 6 g.

GARLIC PEPPER BREAKFAST SAUSAGE
. . . . . .

A savory sausage which can also be made with ground turkey or chicken.

1 pound/454 g ground raw pork
1¹/₂ tsp/7.5 ml Watkins Sage
1 tsp/5 ml ground Watkins Garlic Peppercorn Blend
¹/₂ tsp/2.5 ml salt

Combine all ingredients. Shape into six patties. Cook in large nonstick skillet over medium-high heat, 5 to 7 minutes per side.

Makes 6 servings.

NUTRITIONAL INFORMATION PER SERVING: Calories 210, Protein 25 g, Carbohydrates 0 g, Fat 11 g, Sat Fat 4 g, Cholesterol 80 mg, Sodium 234 mg, Dietary Fiber 0 g.

CROWN OF LAMB ROAST
WITH APPLE STUFFING
· · · · · ·

This elegant classic is perfect for Easter or Christmas, served with roasted potatoes, steamed green beans or baby carrots, and a dry red *Côtes du Rhône*.

1 crown of lamb roast
(approx. 4 pounds/1.8 kg)*
1 tsp/5 ml salt
1 tsp/5 ml Watkins Black Pepper
1 tsp/5 ml Watkins Garlic Flakes
6 tbsp/90 ml butter
1 tbsp/15 ml Watkins Onion Flakes
1 tbsp/15 ml Watkins Poultry Seasoning
1/2 tsp/2.5 ml salt
1/4 tsp/0.6 ml Watkins Black Pepper
1 cup/250 ml chopped celery
3 cups/750 ml dry bread cubes
3 cups/750 ml chopped unpeeled red apple
1/2 cup/125 ml chopped walnuts
Bacon or side pork

Rub roast with salt, pepper, and garlic flakes; place in large shallow roasting pan. In large skillet, melt butter and sauté onion flakes about 1 minute. Remove from heat and add poultry seasoning, salt and pepper; mix well. Add celery, bread cubes, apples and nuts; mix lightly but thoroughly. Fill roast with apple stuffing. Place bacon or pork on top of rib ends to prevent charring. Cover top of roast and stuffing lightly with foil. Roast at 350°F./180°C. for 30 to 35 minutes per pound. Using two spatulas, move to serving platter. Remove bacon and replace with paper frills. Allow 2 ribs per serving.

Makes 8 servings.

*Note from kitchen: Call your butcher or local meat department in advance, as they may have to special-order or take time to prepare this roast.

NUTRITIONAL INFORMATION PER SERVING: Calories 710, Protein 63 g, Carbohydrates 18 g, Fat 42 g, Sat Fat 19 g, Cholesterol 220 mg, Sodium 820 mg, Dietary Fiber 2 g.

CHILI STEAK WITH CORN SALSA
· · · · · ·

Southwestern food fans will love this spicy steak, served with a
zesty, crunchy salsa.

1 tbsp/15 ml Watkins Chili Powder
1 tbsp/15 ml Watkins Cumin
1¹/₂ tsp/7.5 ml Watkins Garlic Salt
1¹/₂ tsp/7.5 ml Watkins Cajun Pepper
4 rib eye steaks (about 6 oz/170 g each)

Combine first four ingredients and rub into steaks; refrigerate
until ready to cook. Grill or broil 4 inches from heat to
desired doneness. Serve with Corn Salsa (recipe follows).

Makes 4 servings.

NUTRITIONAL INFORMATION PER SERVING: Calories 490, Protein 44 g, Carbohydrates 3 g, Fat 33 g, Sat Fat 13 g,
Cholesterol 130 mg, Sodium 690 mg, Dietary Fiber 1 g.

CORN SALSA
· · · · · ·

2 cups/500 ml frozen corn, thawed
¹/₄ cup/60 ml chopped red or green bell pepper
2 tbsp/30 ml sliced green onions
4 tsp/20 ml lime juice
1 tbsp/15 ml Watkins Jalapeño Mustard, more if desired
2 tsp/10 ml honey
¹/₂ to ³/₄ tsp/5 to 7.5 ml Watkins Cilantro, to taste
Watkins Cajun Pepper, to taste

Combine all ingredients in medium bowl; mix well.

Makes 4 servings.

NUTRITIONAL INFORMATION PER SERVING: Calories 90, Protein 3 g, Carbohydrates 22 g, Fat 0 g, Sat Fat 0 g,
Cholesterol 0 mg, Sodium 120 mg, Dietary Fiber 4 g.

ROYAL PEPPERCORN BEEF KEBABS
· · · · · ·

Serve over a bed of rice. Accompany with a fresh lettuce salad.

1 pound/454 g well-trimmed beef top sirloin,
  1¹/₂ inches/4 cm thick
1¹/₂ tsp/7.5 ml crushed Royal Pepper Blend*
1 tsp/5 ml Watkins Grill Seasoning
¹/₂ tsp/2.5 ml Watkins Garlic Powder
1 large onion, cut into 8 wedges
4 cherry tomatoes

Cut beef into 1¹/₄-inch/3-cm pieces. Combine Royal Pepper, Grill Seasoning, and garlic powder in shallow bowl. Add beef cubes and toss to coat well. Thread equally onto four 12-inch/30-cm metal or wooden skewers along with onion wedges. Top each with cherry tomato. Place on grill or broiler pan so surface of meat is 3 to 5 inches from heat. Grill or broil until desired doneness.

Makes 4 servings.

*Note from kitchen: To easily crush pepper, place in a small plastic bag and pound with the flat side of a meat mallet or with the bottom of a heavy saucepan.

NUTRITIONAL INFORMATION PER SERVING: Calories 250, Protein 33 g, Carbohydrates 4 g, Fat 10 g, Sat Fat 4 g, Cholesterol 90 mg, Sodium 340 mg, Dietary Fiber 1 g.

GRILLED GARLIC PEPPER STEAK WITH ZESTY BARBECUE BUTTER

· · · · · ·

Did you really need an excuse to fire up the grill again? This is "guy food" full of bold, manly flavors; it will be one of Dad's favorites.

2 pounds/908 g sirloin steak
2 tsp/10 ml Watkins Garlic Peppercorn Blend,
*   coarsely cracked**

_____

¹/₂ cup/125 ml butter, softened
1¹/₂ tbsp/25 ml Watkins Bold Barbecue Sauce Concentrate
1¹/₂ tsp/7.5 ml Watkins Parsley
¹/₈ tsp/0.6 ml Watkins Garlic Powder

Sprinkle the garlic pepper evenly over steak; press in with fingertips. Let stand 30 minutes. Meanwhile, combine butter and remaining ingredients; beat until smooth. Place in small bowl; set aside. Grill or broil steak until desired doneness. Cut into serving-size pieces; serve with butter.

Makes 6 servings.

*Tip: To coarsely crack pepper, place in small plastic bag and hit with the bottom of a heavy pan or with a meat mallet.

NUTRITIONAL INFORMATION PER SERVING: Calories 450, Protein 44 g, Carbohydrates 42 g, Fat 29 g, Sat Fat 15 g, Cholesterol 157 mg, Sodium 340 mg, Dietary Fiber 0 g.

PEPPERED BEEF TENDERLOIN WITH SAUTÉED MUSHROOMS AND ONION

· · · · · ·

Serve this mouth-watering dish with roasted potatoes and a fresh lettuce salad.

4 beef tenderloin steaks (filets mignons), each 1 inch/2.5 cm
   thick and about 6 oz/170 g
1¹/₂ tsp/7.5 ml Watkins Cracked Black Pepper
³/₄ tsp/7.5 ml Watkins Garlic Salt
1 tbsp/15 ml vegetable oil
1 package (8 oz/227 g) sliced fresh mushrooms
1 small onion, sliced
2 tbsp/30 ml red wine vinegar
3 tbsp/45 ml water
2 tsp/10 ml all-purpose flour
1¹/₂ tsp/7.5 ml Watkins Beef Soup Base

Sprinkle steaks evenly with cracked pepper and garlic salt.
Heat a nonstick skillet over medium-high heat until very
hot. Cook steaks 5 minutes; turn and cook 4 to 5 minutes
longer for rare or until desired doneness. Remove to a
platter to keep warm.

Add oil to drippings in skillet. Add mushrooms and onions
and cook, stirring frequently, until mushrooms are golden
and onion is tender and all liquid has evaporated. In a cup,
mix together the vinegar and next three ingredients; stir into
mushroom mixture and cook until mixture begins to boil and
thicken. Spoon mushroom mixture over steaks. Garnish
with fresh parsley.

Makes 4 servings.

NUTRITIONAL INFORMATION PER SERVING: Calories 390, Protein 50 g, Carbohydrates 7 g, Fat 17 g, Sat Fat 6 g,
Cholesterol 130 mg, Sodium 510 mg, Dietary Fiber 2 g.

P E P P E R

BIFTECK AU POIVRE
(PEPPERED STEAK)
· · · · · ·

Perhaps the definitive black pepper recipe, this classic can be made as spicy as you like by adjusting the amount of pepper used.

2 to 3 pounds/908 to 1360 g T-bone or other choice steak
(about 1¹/₂ inches/4 cm thick)
2 tsp/10 ml Watkins Cracked Black Pepper
¹/₂ tsp/2.5 ml salt, if desired
¹/₈ tsp/0.6 ml Watkins Onion Powder
¹/₈ tsp/0.6 ml Watkins Garlic Powder

Trim fat from steak. Combine pepper and remaining ingredients. Sprinkle evenly over both sides of steak, pressing down firmly with hand or spatula. Let stand ¹/₂ hour; cook 4 to 5 inches from coals or broiler until done to your taste. Cut into serving pieces.

Makes 4 to 6 servings.

NUTRITIONAL INFORMATION PER SERVING: Calories 450, Protein 44 g, Carbohydrates 2g, Fat 29 g, Sat Fat 15 g, Cholesterol 160 mg, Sodium 340 mg, Dietary Fiber 0 g.

ROYAL PEPPER BEEF TENDERLOIN

· · · · · ·

Serve this very juicy, tender cut of meat for special occasions. Although the addition of ginger, garlic and soy sauce may seem Oriental, Asian cuisines are not terribly big on beef. These ingredients, together with pepper, have nonetheless found their way into many traditional English and American beef marinades. This recipe will taste hauntingly familiar, but better than you remember.

1 beef tenderloin (about 2 pounds/908 g)
1 tbsp/15 ml coarsely crushed Watkins Royal Pepper Blend
1 tsp/5 ml Watkins Ginger
1 tsp/5 ml Watkins Garlic Powder
1/4 cup/60 ml soy sauce
Vegetable cooking spray

Trim fat from tenderloin. Combine the Royal Pepper, ginger, and garlic powder. Rub into all sides of tenderloin. Place in a large zipper-type plastic bag. Pour soy sauce over the top. Seal bag and let marinate in refrigerator 8 hours, turning bag occasionally.

Remove tenderloin from bag, reserving marinade. Fold under 3 to 4 inches/8 to 10 cm of small end to achieve uniform thickness. Place tenderloin on a broiler rack coated with cooking spray. Insert a meat thermometer into thickest portion of tenderloin. Roast at 425°F./220°C. for 40 to 45 minutes or until meat thermometer registers 140°F./60°C. (rare) or 160°F./70°C. (medium), basting frequently with reserved marinade.

Place tenderloin on serving platter; let stand 10 minutes before slicing. Garnish with fresh parsley and orange slices.

Makes 8 servings.

NUTRITIONAL INFORMATION PER SERVING: Calories 240, Protein 33 g, Carbohydrates 1 g, Fat 10 g, Sat Fat 4 g, Cholesterol 87 mg, Sodium 590 mg, Dietary Fiber 0 g.

NEW ORLEANS-STYLE HAMBURGERS
· · · · · ·

You'll love the spicy Cajun flavor of these juicy burgers.

1¹/₂ *pounds/680 g lean ground beef*
3 *tbsp/45 ml Watkins Parisienne Mustard*
1 *tsp/5 ml Watkins Cajun Pepper, divided*
1 *tsp/5 ml Watkins Garlic Salt, divided*
³/₄ *tsp/4 ml Watkins Thyme*
¹/₂ *tsp/2.5 ml Watkins Oregano*
1 *large onion, sliced*
1 *large green pepper, sliced*
1 *loaf French bread, cut into 6 slices to fit burgers,*
  split in half
1 *large tomato, sliced*

In medium bowl, combine ground beef, mustard, ³/₄ tsp/4 ml each Cajun Pepper and garlic salt, thyme, and oregano; mix just until combined. Shape into six oval patties; set aside.

In large nonstick skillet, sauté onions and green peppers along with the remaining ¹/₄ tsp/1.2 ml each of Cajun Pepper and garlic salt over medium heat. Remove from skillet and keep warm. In same skillet, place burgers and cook until they reach desired doneness, turning once. Place burgers on bottom half of bun and top with peppers, onions, and tomato slices.

Makes 6 servings.

NUTRITIONAL INFORMATION PER SERVING: Calories 430, Protein 32 g, Carbohydrates 22 g, Fat 23 g, Sat Fat 9 g, Cholesterol 100 mg, Sodium 700 mg, Dietary Fiber 1 g.

SAUERBRATEN

· · · · · ·

This German specialty is just right for an Oktoberfest party. Pickled red cabbage makes a delicious and colorful accompaniment.

3½ cups/875 ml water
3/4 cup/180 ml red wine vinegar,
   more if desired
2 small onions, sliced
2 tbsp/30 ml Watkins Pickling Spice
2 tbsp/30 ml brown sugar
2 tsp/10 ml Watkins Seasoning Salt
1½ tsp/7.5 ml Watkins Cracked Black Pepper
2 Watkins Bay Leaves
3 pounds/1.4 kg trimmed beef bottom
   round roast
Vegetable cooking spray

SAUCE

· · · · · ·

2½ cups/625 ml reserved marinade
½ cup/125 ml crushed gingersnaps*
½ cup/125 ml sour cream

Combine water and next seven ingredients in a large zipper-lock plastic bag; mix well. Add the roast, making sure that the marinade is evenly distributed on all sides.

Close bag and refrigerate for 1 to 3 days. Remove meat from marinade (reserving marinade) and pat dry with paper toweling. Spray cooking spray in large kettle or Dutch oven; place over medium heat. Brown roast on all sides; add reserved marinade. Bring to a boil; reduce heat and simmer 2½ to 3 hours or until meat is tender. Remove meat to a platter and keep warm.

Strain liquid through a fine mesh strainer. Return 2½ cups/625 ml of these reserved juices to kettle and bring to a boil. Whisk in crushed gingersnaps until smooth and mixture begins to thicken. Reduce heat and stir in sour cream; cook until heated through. (Do not boil.) Serve with dumplings, boiled potatoes, or noodles.

Makes 8 servings.

*A good excuse to make *Pepparkakor* (page 105).

NUTRITIONAL INFORMATION PER SERVING: Calories 430, Protein 52 g, Carbohydrates 20 g, Fat 16 g, Sat Fat 6 g, Cholesterol 124 mg, Sodium 470 mg, Dietary Fiber 0 g.

CORNED BEEF DINNER
. . . . . .

In the United States, Corned Beef and Cabbage has become associated with St. Patrick's Day and Ireland, even though it really originated in England. Serve it with a Guinness Stout, and no one will mind.

3 pounds/1.3 kg corned beef, trimmed of fat
4 cups/1 liter water
1 tbsp/15 ml Watkins Chicken Soup Base
2 tsp/10 ml Watkins Garlic Flakes
1 tsp/5 ml Watkins Cracked Black Pepper
2 Watkins Bay Leaves
8 small new potatoes
4 medium carrots, peeled and quartered
4 small boiling onions, halved
3 small turnips, peeled and cut into eighths
1 small head cabbage, cut into wedges
Horseradish Mustard Sauce (recipe follows)

Place corned beef and next five ingredients in large kettle or Dutch oven; bring mixture to a boil. Cover and reduce heat; simmer for 2½ hours or until meat is tender.

Remove meat from kettle and keep warm. Add potatoes, carrots, onions, and turnips to water in kettle; add more water if necessary to cover vegetables. Bring to a boil, then simmer gently for 15 minutes. Add cabbage wedges and continue to simmer for an additional 10 to 15 minutes or until vegetables are tender; remove from water with slotted spoon. To serve, slice meat into thin slices and place on serving platter. Surround meat with vegetables. Drizzle a small amount of the Horseradish Mustard Sauce over meat, serving remainder on the side.

Makes 8 servings.

HORSERADISH MUSTARD SAUCE
. . . . . .

½ cup/125 ml Watkins Cream Soup Base
½ cup/125 ml all-purpose flour
1 cup/250 ml milk
1½ cups/375 ml water
¼ cup/60 ml Watkins Horseradish Mustard
1½ tsp/7.5 ml Watkins Dry Mustard

Combine all ingredients in medium saucepan; bring to a boil, stirring occasionally, until mixture begins to thicken. Serve hot.

Makes 3 cups/750 ml.

NUTRITIONAL INFORMATION PER SERVING: Calories 490, Protein 27 g, Carbohydrates 36 g, Fat 27 g, Sat Fat 8 g, Cholesterol 120 mg, Sodium 2107 mg, Dietary Fiber 6 g.

DESSERTS

BLACK PEPPER SPICE CAKE
· · · · ·

A moist spice cake with a fluffy caramel frosting.

2¹/₂ cups/625 ml sifted cake flour
1 tsp/5 ml Watkins Baking Powder
1 tsp/5 ml salt
³/₄ tsp/4 ml baking soda
³/₄ tsp/4 ml Watkins Ground Cloves
³/₄ tsp/4 ml Watkins Cinnamon
¹/₄ tsp/1.2 ml Watkins Black Pepper
1¹/₂ tsp/7.5 ml Watkins Vanilla Extract
³/₄ cup/180 ml vegetable shortening
1 cup/250 ml white sugar
³/₄ cup/180 ml brown sugar
3 eggs
1 cup/250 ml sour milk

Sift together the first three ingredients; set aside. Combine soda and next five ingredients; mix well. Gradually blend in sugars; beating until well-combined. Beat in eggs, one at a time. Alternately add half of the flour mixture, then half of the sour milk; repeat using remaining flour and milk. Turn batter into three well-greased and lightly-floured 9-inch/23-cm round cake pans. Bake at 375°F./190°C. for 25 minutes. Cool 10 minutes in pans. Turn out of pans onto wire rack and cool completely.

FROSTING
· · · · ·

1¹/₂ cups/375 ml brown sugar
2 large egg whites
¹/₄ cup/60 ml water
¹/₂ tsp/2.5 ml Watkins Nutmeg
¹/₄ tsp/1.2 ml cream of tartar
¹/₈ tsp/0.6 ml salt
1¹/₂ tsp/7.5 ml Watkins Caramel Flavor
1 tsp/5 ml Watkins Vanilla Extract

Place sugar and next five ingredients in top of double boiler. Beat with electric mixer until well blended. Place pan over bottom pan containing 2 inches/5 cm of boiling water. Beat with electric mixer until frosting stands in soft peaks. Remove top of pan from heat. Add caramel flavor and vanilla. Continue to beat until stiff peaks form. Use to frost between layers and on top and sides of cake.

Makes 12 servings.

NUTRITIONAL INFORMATION PER SERVING: Calories 450, Protein 5 g, Carbohydrates 74 g, Fat 15 g, Sat Fat 4 g, Cholesterol 56 mg, Sodium 330 mg, Dietary Fiber 1 g.

ROSEMARY BISCOTTI

· · · · · ·

Originally unknown outside of Italy, these crunchy, twice-baked cookies are a big hit in American coffee houses, restaurants, and bakeries. Serve as an appetizer with cheese and wine, or as a savory dessert with coffee or a dessert wine.

¹/₄ cup/60 ml butter, softened
2 tbsp/30 ml olive oil
2 cups/500 ml all-purpose flour, divided
¹/₃ cup/80 ml white sugar
2 eggs
1¹/₂ tsp/7.5 ml Watkins Rosemary, crushed
2 tsp/10 ml Watkins Baking Powder
¹/₂ tsp/2.5 ml Watkins Black Pepper
¹/₄ cup/60 ml chopped slivered almonds

In large mixing bowl, beat butter and olive oil until softened. Add 1 cup/250 ml of the flour, sugar, eggs, rosemary, baking powder, and pepper; beat until combined. Stir in remaining flour and slivered almonds. Divide dough in half. Shape each half into a log 6 inches/15 cm long and 2 inches/5 cm wide. Place the logs about 4 inches/10 cm apart on a lightly-greased baking sheet. Bake at 375°F./190°C. for 25 minutes. Cool on cookie sheet on wire rack for 1 hour.

With a serrated knife, cut each log into ¹/₂-inch/1-cm-thick slices. Place cut side down on ungreased baking sheet. Bake slices at 325°F./165°C. for 12 minutes. Turn slices over and bake an additional 8 to 10 minutes or until dry and crisp. Transfer from cookie sheet to wire rack to cool. Store in an air-tight container for up to 2 weeks or keep in freezer for up to 16 months.

Makes 20 biscotti, 1 per serving.

NUTRITIONAL INFORMATION PER SERVING: Calories 70, Protein 1 g, Carbohydrates 5 g, Fat 5 g, Sat Fat 2 g, Cholesterol 28 mg, Sodium 60 mg, Dietary Fiber 0 g.

PEPPER

PEPPARKAKOR

· · · · · ·

Black pepper gives the extra flavor "zing" to these Swedish gingersnaps, a version of which may be found in every Scandinavian country, particularly at Christmas. Perhaps they provide that extra warmth to help one get through a cold Solstice night near the Arctic Circle.

1/2 cup/125 ml unsalted butter
1/2 cup/125 ml brown sugar
1/4 cup/60 ml light molasses
2 tsp/10 ml Watkins Cinnamon
2 tsp/10 ml Watkins Ginger
1 tsp/5 ml Watkins Cloves
1 tsp/5 ml Watkins Black Pepper
1 tsp/5 ml baking soda
2 tbsp/30 ml cream or milk
2 cups/500 ml all-purpose flour

In a large bowl, beat butter and next seven ingredients until blended. Beat in cream, then flour, just until blended. Chill 30 minutes or until firm enough to handle.

Shape dough into ³/₄-inch/2-cm balls. Press down lightly with a floured or sugared glass. Bake at 350°F./180°C. for 8 to 10 minutes or until lightly browned. Cool on baking sheet 1 minute then transfer to wire rack to cool completely. If desired, cookies can be drizzled with melted vanilla chips.

Makes about 6 dozen, 1 per serving.

NUTRITIONAL INFORMATION PER SERVING: Calories 30, Protein 0 g, Carbohydrates 5 g, Fat 1 g, Sat Fat 1 g, Cholesterol 4 mg, Sodium 10 mg, Dietary Fiber 0 g.

PEPPERED ORANGE-WALNUT BISCOTTI
· · · · · ·

Serve this tasty crisp cookie with a robust cup of espresso or sweet dessert wine.

1³/₄ cups/440 ml all-purpose flour
¹/₂ tsp/2.5 ml baking soda
¹/₂ tsp/2.5 ml Watkins Baking Powder
¹/₈ tsp/0.6 ml salt
1¹/₂ tsp/7.5 ml Watkins Black Pepper
¹/₂ cup/125 ml unsalted butter, softened
1 cup/250 ml white sugar
2 large eggs, room temperature
2 tsp/10 ml Watkins Orange Extract
1 tsp/5 ml Watkins Vanilla Extract
1¹/₂ cups/375 ml walnuts, lightly toasted
    and coarsely chopped

In medium bowl, combine first five ingredients; set aside. In large bowl, cream butter and sugar until light and fluffy. Mix in eggs one at a time. Mix in extracts. Mix in walnuts. Add dry ingredients and mix just until blended. Cover dough with plastic wrap and refrigerate until well chilled. (Can be prepared 1 day ahead.)

Butter and flour two baking sheets. Divide dough into 2 pieces. Using lightly floured hands, shape each piece into a 1¹/₂-inch/4-cm-wide log on a lightly floured surface. Arrange each on baking sheet. Bake at 350°F./180°C. for 20 minutes or until logs are light brown. Cool slightly on pan.

Cut logs on baking sheet crosswise on diagonal into ³/₄-inch/2-cm-wide slices. Turn cut side down on baking sheet. Bake until golden brown, about 15 minutes. Transfer to racks and cool. Store in airtight container.

Makes 3¹/₂ dozen, 1 per serving.

NUTRITIONAL INFORMATION PER SERVING: Calories 90, Protein 1 g, Carbohydrates 10 g, Fat 5 g, Sat Fat 2 g, Cholesterol 16 mg, Sodium 24 mg, Dietary Fiber 0 g.

HOT AND COOL ICE CREAM
· · · · · ·

The name of this ice cream says it all. The heat from the pepper provides a
wonderful accompaniment to this rich-tasting ice cream.

1¹/₂ cups/375 ml half-and-half
¹/₂ cup/125 ml cream of coconut
¹/₂ cup/125 ml white sugar, divided
2 egg yolks
1 tsp/5 ml Watkins Vanilla Extract
*1 tsp/5 ml coarsely crushed Watkins Royal Pepper Blend,
    divided*

In medium saucepan, combine half-and-half, cream of
coconut, and ¹/₄ cup/60 ml sugar. Heat over medium heat to
a simmer. Combine egg yolks and remaining ¹/₄ cup/60 ml
sugar. Gradually whisk a little of the hot cream mixture into
egg yolks. Return this mixture to remaining cream in
saucepan and cook, stirring constantly, until mixture begins
to coat back of spoon (about 5 minutes). Do not boil.
Remove from heat and add vanilla and ¹/₂ tsp/2.5 ml of the
Royal Pepper; let stand 5 minutes.

Strain custard through a fine sieve into a clean bowl.
Cover and refrigerate about 2 hours. Stir in the
remaining ¹/₂ tsp/5 ml Royal Pepper. Freeze according
to ice cream maker's instructions.

Makes 2¹/₂ cups/625 ml, 5 servings.

NUTRITIONAL INFORMATION PER SERVING: Calories 280, Protein 4 g, Carbohydrates 25 g, Fat 19 g, Sat Fat 13 g,
Cholesterol 112 mg, Sodium 34 mg, Dietary Fiber 0 g.

PEPPER

STRAWBERRIES
WITH BALSAMIC VINEGAR
· · · · · ·

Walking the line between sweet and savory, this dessert pulls together the heat
of pepper and the sweetness of strawberries with the help of balsamic vinegar.
A product of Modena, Italy, this intensely-flavored yet mellow, dark, sweet vinegar
is made by aging the juice of sweet white grapes for years (sometimes decades!)
through a succession of wooden barrels. This is a breakfast favorite in Italy
(but we added the pepper).

1 quart/1 liter fresh strawberries, hulled and sliced
6 tbsp/90 ml balsamic vinegar
2 tbsp/30 ml white sugar
$1/4$ tsp/1.2 ml coarsely ground Watkins Cracked Black Pepper

Toss strawberries with vinegar, sugar, and pepper. Serve
immediately.

Makes 6 servings.

NUTRITIONAL INFORMATION PER SERVING: Calories 50, Protein 1 g, Carbohydrates 12 g, Fat 0 g, Sat Fat 0 g,
Cholesterol 0 mg, Sodium 1 mg, Dietary Fiber 3 g.

PFEFFERNUSSE (PEPPERNUTS)
· · · · · ·

These spice cookies are even better when allowed to mellow for several days
in a tightly closed container.

2 cups/500 ml all-purpose flour
3/4 tsp/4 ml Watkins Cinnamon
3/4 tsp/4 ml Watkins Baking Powder
3/4 tsp/4 ml Watkins Allspice
3/4 tsp/4 ml salt
3/4 tsp/4 ml Watkins Nutmeg
1/2 tsp/2.5 ml Watkins Black Pepper
1 cup/250 ml honey
3 tbsp/45 ml vegetable shortening
1 egg

Sift together all dry ingredients. Heat the honey but do
not boil; add shortening and allow to cool. Beat in the
egg. Stir in dry ingredients just until blended. Let dough
stand 10 minutes to stiffen enough to handle. Shape into
1 1/2-inch/4-cm balls. Bake at 350°F./180°C. for 10 to 12
minutes. If desired, cookies can be frosted (recipe follows.)

Makes 6 dozen, 1 per serving.

NUTRITIONAL INFORMATION PER SERVING (plain): Calories 30, Protein 0 g, Carbohydrates 7 g, Fat 1 g, Sat Fat 0 g,
Cholesterol 3 mg, Sodium 30 mg, Dietary Fiber 0 g.

FROSTING
· · · · · ·

1 1/2 cups/375 ml powdered sugar
2 tbsp/30 ml butter
3/4 tsp/4 ml Watkins Vanilla Extract
1 tbsp/15 ml milk

Combine all ingredients and mix until smooth.

NUTRITIONAL INFORMATION PER SERVING (frosted): Calories 40, Protein 1 g, Carbohydrates 9 g, Fat 1 g, Sat Fat 0 g,
Cholesterol 4 mg, Sodium 30 mg, Dietary Fiber 0 g.

P E P P E R

ROYAL PEPPER COOKIES

· · · · · ·

The sharpness of pepper and the roundness of vanilla complement each other beautifully in these buttery cookies. Like Mom's sugar cookies with a surprising twist.

2¹/₄ cups/560 ml all-purpose flour
1 cup/250 ml white sugar
1 cup/250 ml butter, softened
1 egg
1 tsp/5 ml baking soda
1 tsp/5 ml Watkins Vanilla Extract
1¹/₂ tsp/7.5 ml coarsely crushed Watkins Royal Pepper Blend
Watkins Royal Pepper Blend (whole peppercorns), for garnish

Combine all ingredients except whole peppercorns; mix well. Roll into ¹/₂-inch/1-cm balls. Place on ungreased cookie sheet. Press flat with a buttered glass that has been dipped in sugar. Place a peppercorn in center of each. Bake at 350°F./180°C. for 8 to 11 minutes or until lightly golden around edges. Remove cookies to wire rack to cool.

Makes 4 dozen, 1 per serving.

NUTRITIONAL INFORMATION PER SERVING: Calories 70, Protein 1 g, Carbohydrates 9 g, Fat 4 g, Sat Fat 2 g, Cholesterol 15 mg, Sodium 50 mg, Dietary Fiber 0 g.

INDEX